Praise for
How to Get Clients:

"Steve Chandler's *How to Get Clients* is one of the most important books you will ever read. It shows you how to fill your coaching practice in a way that doesn't require selling, marketing, or manipulating. You can be highly sought-after just by being more of who you truly are and by focusing on how to genuinely help others (whether they end up being your clients or not). I can't recommend a business book more highly. What's more, it's a darn entertaining and funny read."

~ **Mark Levy,** author of *Accidental Genius*

"*How to Get Clients* is THE operating manual for how to create a prosperous, sustainable and thriving practice. Having attended Steve's live Coaching Prosperity School five times and created a magnificent coaching business, I saw new insights and practices in this book that I am adding immediately, and which will help me and the coaches I serve grow to our next level. In Steve's storytelling there is an authenticity and transparency that provides hope and a roadmap to prosperity. A MUST READ for all coaches and consultants!"

~ **Kamin Samuel,** author of *Increase Your Abundance Starting Today*

"Simple, clear, direct! Steve Chandler has done it again with this powerful, practical book setting forth the basic operating principles that ALL prosperous coaches use to create clients. Any coach who is serious about running a thriving coaching business must read (often), test (repeatedly) and integrate these new pathways to prosperity."

~ **Melissa Ford,** author of *Living Service*

"Chandler's humor (which is the ironic type I like so much) comes through page after page. But the humor is just the wrapper for the undeniably rich content. This book is rich in 'how-to' live this and be a person of service. I know this book is intended for life coaches (and other types of coaches), but it is really for anyone who wants clients or sales orders or customers—or anything else they need but don't have in their world."

~ **William Keiper,** author of *Untethered Aging*

"Inside *How to Get Clients* Steve Chandler artfully shares a blend of beautifully written, real-world anecdotes with insightful client-creation principles that have helped launch the career of some of the most financially successful coaches on the planet today. If you truly want to master the art of selling without selling then read this book—cover to cover and in-between the lines—to take in priceless wisdom from THE ORIGINAL MASTER COACH. If you do this and practice what Steve offers, you'll create professional prosperity AND enhance every relationship in your life."

~ **David Foster,** author of *Where's Dad?*

How to Get Clients

How to Get Clients

New Pathways to Coaching Prosperity

STEVE CHANDLER

MAURICE BASSETT

How to Get Clients: New Pathways to Coaching Prosperity

Maurice Bassett
P.O. Box 839
Anna Maria, FL 34216

Contact the publisher:
MauriceBassett@gmail.com

Contact the author:
www.SteveChandler.com

Editing: Kathy Eimers Chandler and Chris Nelson
Cover design: Carrie Brito

ISBN: 978-1-60025-161-0

Library of Congress Control Number: 2021936973

Revised Edition

Table of Contents

Foreword: A vital and magical way to learn 13

Introduction: My coaching career was built on a deception..........17

1. Nobody wants coaching...................................25
2. People don't want coaching; they want possibility 28
3. Okay, but how do I get clients? 32
4. Am I a moron, or am I just confused? 37
5. What if bad advice is all you've got? 43
6. Unbelievable missed opportunities....................49
7. One more river to cross................................53
8. But on the other hand 59
9. Base yourself on infinite possibilities................65
10. You can *create* a future full of clients 69
11. Habits disguise themselves as traits
    and characteristics.....................................73
12. Imagine no more failed sales calls....................76
13. I couldn't deal with "rejection" 80
14. Where should my attention be today? 84
15. Willing to revisit priorities...........................88
16. Show me your calendar! 94
17. Commitment to client cultivation 97
18. Blooming and flourishing as a coach.................102
19. Is there a right way to get clients? 106
20. What if people DO want coaching?...................110
21. Curiosity is the ultimate power......................114
22. Give them CONTENT, not concept! 123

23. Remember who you really are 127

24. People want to help you get clients 135

25. What if I have no one to talk to? 144

26. When searching for clients disappears 151

27. From referrals to renewals to prosperity 160

Recommended Resources for Coaches 169

Bonus Chapters from CREATOR 171

About the author 187

Books by Steve Chandler 189

Audio by Steve Chandler 191

Steve Chandler Coaching Prosperity School 193

Acknowledgments

So many thanks to my life's mentor, the ultimate coach, Steve Hardison, without whom nothing like this book, our school or my career would have happened.

To my publisher and gifted, service-oriented Director of the ACS, Maurice Bassett.

To Kathy for her love and support and humor and for showing me all things true and beautiful along the path.

To our brilliant editor Chris Nelson; to the artistic Carrie Brito; and to my guest teachers in the Coaching Prosperity School whose wisdom and guidance I will continue to draw from: Michael Neill, Carolyn Freyer-Jones, Rich Litvin, Tom Chi, Karen Davis, Devon Bandison, Kamin Samuel, Jason Goldberg, Ankush Jain, Tina Quinn, Stephen McGhee, Ron Wilder, Melissa Ford, Siawash Zahmat, Alex Mill, and Teena Goble.

To singer-songwriter Fred Knipe for all-around great advice throughout the project, and to Mark Levy, differentiation expert and author of *Accidental Genius: Using Writing to Generate Your Best Ideas, Insight, and Content* for creatively inspired help with both the Prosperity School online version and this book, which is derived from the teachings at that school.

To Kathy

Foreword

A vital and magical way to learn

Steve Chandler has been my coach for over fifteen years. His influence in my whole life and on my success as a professional coach cannot be overstated. Everything I have learned about how to create a financially successful coaching practice, I learned from Steve.

Everything I learned about how to connect, to slow down and to build relationships, I learned from Steve. Everything about how to make a difference, to give and give more without any thought of getting, I learned from Steve.

Steve Chandler has transformed my life and made my work as a professional coach in the world better than I could have ever imagined—and he did it over and over and over, again and again and again. He'll likely do it again tomorrow.

How to Get Clients is a vital and magical way to have Steve make a difference in your work as a coach, no matter where you are on the journey. Steve Chandler is not just a master in the art of enrollment—he's THE master.

This profession is far better because of him and his very real, grounded and profound guidance on building a successful business.

Carolyn Freyer-Jones
Los Angeles, California
March, 2021

How to Get Clients

New Pathways to Coaching Prosperity

What a caterpillar calls the end of the world
we call a butterfly.

~ **Eckhart Tolle**

Introduction

My coaching career was built on a deception

B ack at the beginning, I never had a passion for coaching, for changing the world or even for helping others.

I never wanted to help *anyone* (other than my immediate family, although they might "not remember" that if you interview them, so don't interview them; it won't get you any clients to do that, and this book works better for readers who dive in and don't do a lot of extra stuff while reading it all the way to the end).

My entry into the world of coaching was not a dream come true. It was not me discovering my calling, or me finally aligning with the universe and discovering my north star or "zone of genius." The "zone" I entered was better described as a terrifying and miserable twilight zone.

Because I fell into it by accident (that is, if a shameless deception can be ruled an accident).

It was decades ago, and I'd been teaching seminars to companies, nonprofits and other organizations on how to get customers, donors and clients using a system I'd co-created with the ace fundraiser Michael Bassoff (more on that system as this story unfolds and/or unravels.)

A medical and hospital group in La Jolla, California, had heard about my seminars and asked me if my system might apply to recruiting nurses. There was a great nationwide shortage of nurses at that time and their hospitals and medical centers were having a hard time bringing them in.

I was drowning in debt back then, and banks were telling me to cut my credit cards in half even as they handed me new ones, and I was taking any seminar job I could get. So I smoothly said, "My system? Absolutely it will help." And to my grateful surprise, after interviewing some of their nurse recruiters I could see that it would at least not be hard to write a seminar proposal that tailored my system to their challenge.

After they reviewed the proposal, they called me right away to hire me. That night I was high-fiving myself in the mirror. The next day we chose a date for me to fly out to

La Jolla to do a day-long workshop with their recruiting team of eight people.

That's when I carelessly abandoned some integrity. (What little I had at the time.)

As we talked over the date and time for the seminar their team leader asked if I would stay over an extra day and "coach" each recruiter individually. They said they had a nice little conference room for me and they'd send each person in one at a time for their hour of coaching.

I was about to politely decline and tell them I didn't know anything about coaching. I'd never done it! No clue *how* to do it. But then the team leader said, "We'll pay you the same fee for that day as we're paying for your seminar day."

Well, now!! Judging from the knee-jerk reaction of both of my knees to the words *"We'll pay you . . ."* the next words I heard myself say couldn't be stopped:

"Yes, absolutely. Coaching? Sure, I can do that! I can do that quite well."

Because, you know, why not, right? They were offering a nice fee. And I was, as I mentioned, dealing with creditors day and night. Some of my creditors were coming to my seminars (by my special invitation) to see for themselves that I was still working for a living and that maybe they would go against their best professional instincts and extend my time allotment to pay them.

Due to multiple previous job failures and family medical setbacks, I had eye-popping old debt. Then there were the *current* bills, arriving almost every day, mainly because I was a broke, single father with full custody of four energetic children who, not satisfied with the shelter and clothing I was providing, kept making additional requests for regular food.

I figured that not knowing how to coach and never having coached before was not a problem for me as long as their check cleared before they had their people enter that little conference room and later fill out the training evaluation forms.

I am pleased to report that I survived that day. For some reason, after the first person sat with me to be coached, they still kept sending people in. I didn't expect that. I feared that the team leader would come in after I'd "coached" that first person and tell me to pack my bags and get out of town.

After I got home, I got an email from the team leader saying that the second day, the "coaching" day, was even better than the first day's seminar. So right then my new career was launched. Or at least the first trial balloon.

But there were still two minor but basic problems at the beginning. One was that I didn't know how to coach, which seems like it would be a major problem. But it wasn't. Because I then immediately committed to ask the most powerful coach I knew of to coach *me* . . . the legendary Steve Hardison. He wouldn't be available for a while, but I knew my sessions with him would show me and teach me how great coaching was done.

My biggest problem was getting clients

The biggest challenge, for me, however, would turn out to be *how to get clients.*

The very thought of that filled me with fear and a strong desire to divide up my client acquisition time between avoidance and aversion. (Not an optimal time management system . . . I was certainly not yet a "time warrior" in that department.)

The truth was that I began to realize I was less equipped to be good at selling myself and this thing called "coaching" than any "coach" I've ever met, before or since. I had deep, near-pathological fears of talking to people about anything that had anything to do with money.

So if I can do a spoiler about the ending of this story, I'll now reveal that my learning to get coaching clients, talk to them about money, and *enjoy doing it* felt somewhat of a miracle. The book that follows will explain how all of it has happened. There actually is a way to do this, and it's a way any coach, new or experienced, can learn and apply immediately.

You'll hear about the internal, spiritual pathways that led to my improbable success. They also have the advantage of having been tested and used successfully by the hundreds of coaches from around the world who have attended a coaching school I eventually taught on how to get clients. It was called the Coaching Prosperity School. (It is now available as an online program.)

I picture my late parents, and some of my old creditors, up in Heaven being told that down on Earth I have been teaching something called "prosperity."

"Where is he teaching it," my father says, after the laughter dies down, "in prison?" And the laughter reignites.

Oh, well. I don't mind laughter. It improves vascular and cognitive, creative function, they say. And any time I write a book that suggests that humor always contains valuable wisdom, I think of a favorite quote of mine by Groucho Marx:

From the moment I picked up your book until I put it down, I was convulsed with laughter. Someday I intend to read it.

I've written a book with Rich Litvin called *The Prosperous Coach*, which gives actionable specifics to coaches on how to get clients. The present book offers what I call vital, internal "operating principles" for client acquisition. When you embody these principles, strategies like those discussed in *The Prosperous Coach* come naturally to mind throughout your day. *How to Get Clients* is written on a more personal level about the internal mind shifts and spiritual upgrades that have occurred for me and so many others, and which can give coaches hope and a new sense of optimism that those actions can be executed without worry or fear. This profession is like any other. No heroics or special courage are needed. And the ultimate proof of that is that if I can do this, you can too.

We have to be practical. If there is something that we can do about a situation then we will do it. But we have to bear in mind that our mission is not to save the world. The world is big, and we are small and frail human beings.

Our mission is to discover genuine happiness and then, when we have discovered it, allow it to overflow and share itself, in an entirely natural fashion, with the rest of the world.

~ Francis Lucille
Eternity Now

1.

Nobody wants coaching

This is the elephant in the room that coaches don't see for a long, long time. But get used to it. It's the truth. And once you can see Dumbo elephant, the less you'll be dumbo the coach.

People don't want coaching.

They want what coaching can do.

They want their problems solved, their habits changed, their opportunities realized.

They want more income, or better relationships, or more peace on the inside, or more fun and adventure on the outside.

They want less suffering and more happiness.

They don't want coaching per se. They don't walk around singing or even thinking, "I want some coaching, just gimme some, gimme some sweet, sweet coaching."

No, that's not what they want. They want the *outcome* of coaching, not the coaching itself. So their minds are on their problems and possible solutions. That's all they want to talk and think about.

It's that. It's not coaching.

But don't get depressed about this, because it's the key to everything you wanted to learn when you bought this book. Knowing that people don't want coaching will free you up from trying to *sell* coaching. You'll see it's like trying to sell skateboards to the patients in your local nursing home.

So when you talk to potential clients, you don't talk about coaching; you talk about *what those people want.* You talk about freedom from fear and suffering, you talk about financial well-being. You talk about an artistically-created future.

And rather than promising breakthroughs, insights and new ideas for a better life, you let them sample it. You offer hope, understanding, freedom, compassion and optimism. You let them sample it ahead of time.

You talk to them.

Because that's what they're going to buy. They're going to buy what happens to them when you talk to them.

I've learned that people will forget what you said, people will forget what you did, but people will never forget how you made them feel.

~ Maya Angelou

2.

People don't want coaching; they want possibility

O nce you understand what your clients really want, you'll learn to spend almost *all* your "sales" and enrollment time talking about what they want. It's all they want to talk about.

If you are in the airport, and you want to change your flight from one going to Chicago to one going to Tampa Bay you go up to the ticket counter and make that request. The attendant works on the computer and finds the next flight and prints up a new ticket and asks for your credit card.

Here's what she *does not do:*

She does not ask you if you'd like to see a video about the plane before you choose the flight. She doesn't invite you to go to the airport auditorium to watch a pilot give a talk about the engines and the aerodynamics that keep your plane flying.

Why?

Because you're not buying the airplane, you're buying the outcome . . . the outcome of you being in Tampa Bay.

I'm spending a lot of time on this because it's a shift in understanding that must happen for you to find the best and fastest pathways to prosperity as a coach.

Why keep trying to sell coaching when that's not (initially) what people want? Yet coaches do that. They sell themselves and they sell coaching. When all the hours and creative energy spent on that useless and exhausting activity *could have been spent talking to someone!*

COACH: I'm not that good at talking to people.

ME: Are you good at listening?

COACH: Well sure, I can do that.

ME: That's great, you're good to go!

Next chapter we'll have fun looking at all the pain, suffering and fear that floods the life of someone trying to sell "coaching" when people don't want it.

I've been there. I've done that. But once I saw how and why that wasn't working to get me clients, I was finally able to relax into what really worked. That's when my practice shifted from a sales and marketing business to a relationship business. And that's when I could breathe.

Anywhere there's a positive difference to be made, there's money to be made. If you can't (or won't) make much of a difference, you're unlikely to make very much money.

~ Michael Neill
Supercoach

3.

Okay, but how do I get clients?

I kept bringing that question to my coach, and at first his answer seemed like he was trying to change the subject.

I thought this subject-changing must have meant that getting clients was as hard for him as it was for me, although when I looked at it clearly I remembered that his practice was full and he had a long waiting list of people who wanted to work with him.

So then why was he giving me this mysterious answer to how I could get clients?

He said, "You learn to get good at selling without selling."

What? That was quite a solution! My first thought was that I could sell that answer to a Zen monastery where they use unsolvable koans like that one ("How do you sell without selling?") to take meditation students out of their minds and into universal consciousness.

One time a Zen practitioner asked me to answer the popular koan, "What is the sound of one hand clapping?" and I held up one hand and snapped my fingers, saying, "*This,* right? Got anything harder?"

I wasn't so cocky about the *selling without selling* koan. How do you sell without selling? Why is that a responsible answer to, "How do I get clients?"

It took a good, long while for me to get what he meant, but once I did, the floodgates opened, and becoming financially strong as a coach had a brand new pathway . . . a road I had never traveled.

So I'll say it here in its short form, and then we'll look at it from all the angles we can think of for how you can use this idea to get clients, build a prosperous practice as a coach, and enjoy the whole thing along the way.

SHORT FORM: You get clients by creating relationships.

Of *course* there's more to it than that. You don't have to get triggered by the simplicity of that and ask for a refund. Not yet, anyway.

The new pathways that lead to prosperity in coaching are going to be more specific, more understandable and more doable than that short form of the book. But as for mindset, you really want to keep that sentence someplace where you can always see it: you get clients by creating relationships.

This is a relationship game.

It's not a selling and marketing game.

Most of the coaches who came to the live version of the Coaching Prosperity School had hit a financial ceiling (sometimes a very low one) by trying to sell, brand, market and promote themselves into prosperity without ever focusing on relationships.

I was just like they were in the beginning of my own career.

Rather than having my coaching day be about creating and cultivating relationships, I had it be about spamming my name and bio and testimonials out into the world, hoping relationships would just eventually happen.

My system was based on my ego. I, me, me, mine. Getting the word out about ME! Building my ego! Build it (my ego) and they will come!

Result? Crickets.

Coaching is private and intimate when it works. There is a feeling of trust and safety. Tooting your own horn in someone's face actually undermines that.

We'll look now at the many ways to replace selling with serving, to replace trying to OVERWHELM someone with learning to invite them into a safe, trusting space full of possibility for the future.

For me and many others, getting clients turns out to be more doable, more relaxing, and more fun than it looks at first. Coaches, especially me in the beginning, often see selling as "awkwardly and shamelessly attempting to bother people, and then trying to take their money."

That was not an activity I ever looked forward to waking up to.

Fortunately, all of that changed. What I feared doing turned into something I loved doing. That made all the difference.

Love is always creative and fear is always destructive. If you could only love enough, you would be the most powerful person in the world.

~ Emmet Fox

4.

Am I a moron,
or am I just confused?

I would tell my own coach at the beginning of my career, "I'm such a moron!"

He would try to make me feel better. He'd say I was just confused.

Confused about what was smart for a coach and what was stupid.

I wanted to have a strong, prosperous career, get out of debt and build some financial security and see if my self-esteem could get its head above the mental quicksand I was living in.

He said, "To make money in this world find someone with a problem and solve it for them."

I tried to tell him that I was already trying to do that.

"No," he said. "You're trying to find someone to whom

you can talk about yourself and your coaching."

He was right.

And it wasn't working.

I was bothering people who didn't know who I was and weren't sure what coaching was, but who knew they didn't want it.

I'd been listening to advisors who said that when you're not getting clients by putting your name out there and becoming better known, you have to increase your attempts to do that. Step it up.

I'd already put too much time and money into websites, email marketing, photographs of me posing with facial expressions that made me look soul-centered and authentic.

I had already stepped up my frantic social media activity, revisions of my personal branding and searching for my niche. I was investing in retreats where I might find my purpose. I paid various motivational entertainers to help me find what they called my "zone of genius."

I found the courage to ask one teacher, "If everyone has a zone of genius, as you say, what does the word 'genius' mean?"

"What do you want it to mean?" he said.

"I want it to mean roughly what the dictionary says it means."

"So you're going to let the dictionary run your life?"

"I think a dictionary helps us to communicate. As we are people who speak with words."

"So maybe you should look into why you get triggered by how a word is being used. I think you should come back to our next retreat, and keep coming back until it's okay with you that everyone is a genius. In their own way. In their own zone."

"I don't think I'm triggered; I think I'm just asking."

"Oh, I think you're triggered. I think maybe you want to be the only genius there is."

I thanked him for the tough talk. But I knew I wasn't a genius, not by the common accepted definition. So it wasn't what I wanted to be. I just wanted to figure out how to make my life work as a coach so that I didn't have all this financial pressure.

And so after the retreat was over, I got back to considering the advice I was getting to step up my marketing and self-promotion. Step it up! How?

I thought of renting one of those little airplanes that fly over the football fields in towns and villages carrying a banner behind the plane with my name on it in bright letters with the word "COACH" before my name. Then I thought of putting the words "MASTER COACH" on the banner in front of my name, but can you really be a master coach if you have few or no clients?

That would be false advertising. Improper use of the airspace. Consider the fine I might have to pay.

Other ideas came to me. I could take a cruise and put my name and phone number on a little piece of cruise line stationery, maybe add a few words like, "Coaching. Awesome experiences!" and put the message into a bottle, cap the bottle and throw it overboard.

Who knows whose beach property it might wash up on? Maybe a millionaire, or even a beachfront billionaire.

As I hope you can see, my mind was headed in the wrong direction. But it was headed in the wrong direction even at the beginning . . . the moment I bought into the advice that said coaches need to advertise and market themselves.

Forget relationships! They come later!

That must be true or else there wouldn't be so many people giving that advice. And even if the advice wasn't bringing results, I tried to make myself believe that bad advice was better than no advice at all.

Then I asked myself, how did I hire my own coach?

Was it because he was famous? No, I'd never heard of him.

Was it because he used hypnotic sales techniques with me? No, he never brought up the idea of me paying for his coaching.

It finally dawned on me that I hired him because I had spent time with him, and every time I had a good, long conversation with him, I felt better. I felt more optimistic. My past, which had always hung over my head like a dark cloud of shame, was not interesting to him. My future, which swarmed around my head like anxious killer bees every time I dared to think about it, was something he saw as filled with possibility.

I hired him because each conversation I had with him left me feeling somehow changed inside. Changed for the better. I began to see real possibility.

I began to understand what the philosopher Kierkegaard meant when he said, "If I were to wish for anything, I should not wish for wealth and power, but for the passionate sense of the potential, for the eye which, ever young and ardent, sees the possible. Pleasure disappoints, possibility never."

There is something in every one of you that waits and listens for the sound of the genuine in yourself. It is the only true guide you will ever have. And if you cannot hear it, you will all of your life spend your days on the ends of strings that somebody else pulls.

~ Howard Thurman

5.

What if bad advice
is all you've got?

And, even more important to ask, "What if all this marketing and self-promotion doesn't work?"

Increase my budget for it? Keep pouring money into it? Until my bank account runneth over? Till the floor is flooded and the house of cards I'm living in gets drenched and falls to the ground?

Back in my days of failure I remembered an old saying that was coming back to me more and more often: *You can never get enough of what you don't need.*

Yes. That is truth. Once I let that in, I was done with spamming, marketing and widespread self-promotion. Another quote came to mind too, a brief quote from Michael LeBoeuf in a book of his I'd read long ago, a book about the habits of millionaires, back when I thought becoming one might be an innovative way to address my debts, a quote I'd underlined that said: "Winners focus, losers spray."

Focus! That started making more sense than the endless quest and spray for professional recognition in the world.

Self-marketing for coaching always felt off . . . and not just because it wasn't helping me get clients. I began to see through to the reason why it wasn't working. It felt like you were telling a single person going to a nice bar in the hope of meeting someone that they needed to jump up on a table and yell out their whole biography and list of good qualities to the room full of people.

I had to admit it. My own personal branding and spam fest was a waste of time in a profession like coaching, a profession that by its very nature values privacy, trust and intimacy. Why did it take me so long to see that?

Failure helped. Failure always helps. I see that now. For a long time I didn't see it. I thought failure was the worst thing. I thought failure was to be avoided at all costs. I thought if I failed it would mean something about me. What's the word I'm looking for?

Oh right, the word is *failure*. If I failed it would mean I was a failure.

Later I saw (and this is one of the benefits of my being coached) that failing at something merely meant that I failed at something. Made more sense. I didn't have to make it my personal identity. It was just something that happened. It wasn't who I was.

If I go to sleep for a while it doesn't mean I'm a "sleeper," and if I fix the backed-up toilet it doesn't mean I'm a plumber, and if I rearrange the books in my office it doesn't mean I'm a librarian . . .

You get where I'm going?

One of my first seminar clients, an entrepreneur who built a hugely successful company from scratch, once said to his sales team in a meeting I was attending, "We are going to fail! Yes we are. But we learn each time we fail, will not be afraid of failing, and so our team motto will always be: FAIL FORWARD!"

Here's a possible light-bulb moment: coaches who in real life are kind, generous and even shy, might not succeed if their marketing and self-promotion portrays them as narcissistic egomaniacs giving endless shout-outs to themselves. Doing so might not help people feel safe in their presence. Especially not a person who values confidentiality and trust. In other words, a potential coaching client.

I began to see that such a communication campaign (one that might work just fine for selling many products and big events) is a total mismatch to the service I was offering: one-on-one coaching.

So I might actually be distancing myself from people with all my dehumanizing attempts to have them see me certain ways without even talking to me.

"Why are you doing all this indirect promotional stuff?" my coach asked one day.

"Well, the idea is to have them ultimately know who I am! And be impressed and intrigued by me over time, so that someday, eventually, maybe down the road, after enough hits, clicks, likes and exposure, they will want to talk to me . . . they'll want to reach out for a conversation . . . about coaching."

"Why don't you just talk to them now? Leave all the rest out?"

I noticed that when my coach wanted to talk to someone he just reached out and talked to them. Even if they didn't know who he was or what he wanted. I also noticed that he had a financially successful practice—and I had the opposite.

It was all starting to add up. No one has ever told me that they chose their coach because of their coach's ego and self-absorption. Not yet, anyway.

People who want *what coaching can do* are put off by all that ear-splitting blowing into my own horn.

This is good news for the coach who is introverted by

habit, and even good news for the extroverted coach who is willing to learn to reach out to people with humility, grace and discretion. And a willingness to cultivate a new, advanced habit called listening.

Once you truly see this (which is why I'm trying to run it into the ground, so it's easier to see) you'll no longer be choosing communication that feels like assault over communication that feels like an embrace.

I was always trying to be impressive with people. It took a long time to realize that people don't really want to be impressed. Not in this profession.

They want to be understood. They want some help. They want to trust that you can hear them, not that they have to keep hearing you.

When we are listened to, it creates us, makes us unfold and expand. Ideas actually begin to grow within us and come to life.

~ **Brenda Ueland**

6.

Unbelievable missed opportunities

I finally really saw that branding my ego was like brandishing a DayGlo skull tattoo around the dark, damp streets of the internet like a carnival barker yelling, "Coaching! Free transformational, life-changing coaching session!"

It wasn't getting me clients. I regrouped.

I started to understand why when I was coaching someone in an organization and I offered a free session to the CEO she almost always said "No, thanks."

That used to bother and confuse me. Why would she pass up an unbelievable opportunity! No cost! Did she hear me right?

She even knew it cost a lot for her to pay me to coach her HR Director. Why would she herself miss this opportunity to be coached by me for free?

But now I could see it. She's like everyone else. She doesn't want coaching.

So after that revelation, I changed the setting on my internal radar. I listened for problems. I scanned for problems . . . places where I might be of help. When I did that, people invited me in to talk, to "brainstorm" solutions to their problem. Neither they nor I called it "coaching" (at the beginning) because coaching (at least at the beginning) was not what they wanted.

They wanted help.

They wanted help, whether they were openly asking for it or not.

Later we would call it "coaching" because by that time the relationship was there. And once the relationship was there, and true differences were occurring inside our initial conversations, the word "coaching" would mean something cool and beautiful to them.

My offering and service, which used to be presented as coaching, had changed overnight from something nobody wanted to something everyone, deep down, wanted.

That's when the problem of *how to get clients* was no longer a problem. It had changed.

My radar was different now. Whereas it was previously set to search out and identify human targets of opportunity—people I could use as a financial means to an end by persuading and manipulating them into being impressed by me and my suspiciously magical love potion I called "coaching"—it was now calibrated to, "Where is there a problem, and how can I help with it?"

To COACH is to encourage:

encourage
verb (used with object)
en·cour·aged, en·cour·ag·ing.

to inspire with courage, spirit, or confidence:

"His coach encouraged him throughout the marathon race to keep on running."

~ dictionary.com

7.

One more river to cross

B ut there was one more myth, one more piece of bad advice consistently given to me (and most other coaches) that had to be deleted.

Many coaching certification programs stress the importance of choosing your niche. You shouldn't proceed without one.

It made me feel stupid and unworthy when I couldn't find one.

In fact I felt even dumber when I had to confess that I didn't even know what a niche was . . . I felt increasingly moronic when I was told by one seminar leader, an experienced teacher, that I wasn't even pronouncing the word correctly.

ME: What exactly *is* a nitch?

EXPERIENCED TEACHER: The word is pronounced "neesh."

ME: Neesh? Like quiche?

ET: Right, it's from the French. We recommend you pronounce it "neesh" so you appear to be more international. You know, not like you're clueless.

ME: Sure. Will do. From now on it's "neesh." But what is it?

ET: It's your category. It's your specialty, as a coach. It's the group of people or the kind of person you're most qualified to coach.

ME: Wow, okay, but do I have to have one? What if I want to coach all different kinds of people . . . all kinds of groups?

ET: No. That's a mistake. A niche is vital. You have to have one. Just like if you're a skydiver, you have to have a parachute, right? Your niche is like a parachute. You don't want to jump into a coaching career without one.

ME: Thanks for the unsettling metaphor, but

you haven't explained exactly why I really need one.

ET: My explanation is this: trust me. *Trust me* is my explanation. It's what I was taught. Remember that when you came to ask me about this you couldn't even pronounce the word. So, baby steps, okay? Don't try to get out ahead of your own evolution.

That was decades ago, but the myth still pervades. In the coaching school I run there are always coaches who confess that they have not decided on their niche yet. They always seem a little ashamed.

I sometimes read to them one of the dictionary definitions of a niche:

"A recess in a wall, especially for a statue." (Merriam-Webster).

That sounds pretty limiting. Not only are you not out there on the floor dancing and talking with others, but you're hidden back in a recess in the wall, or . . . you are a *statue*.

No one wants to create a relationship with a statue. And no one wants to be stranded inside a recess in the wall.

So as I began to see the wisdom of ignoring this myth, I was happy to not restrict or limit my work and service at all.

When I had to put down the niche I'd chosen for ET's class, I put down "Life."

ET: What does this mean? Why did you put down "life" as your niche?

ME: I'm a life coach, right? If I meet someone, and they become interested in my coaching, I check to see if they're alive, and if so I know right away they're in my niche, because my niche is "life." And, so, bingo. Game on. I found someone with a life.

ET: So you couldn't narrow that down?

ME: No, I really don't want to. If I chose a specific group of people for my niche, let's say ballerinas, and I met someone sitting next to me on an airplane, and we're talking about our lives, and she finds out that I coach people, and she says, "I wonder if you could help me with something going on in my business?" I don't want to have to say, "I don't know, are you a ballerina?"

These myths and assumptions, like marketing yourself and finding a niche, lead coaches down the wrong path. They ignore a fundamental truth: this is a relationship business that's moved forward by deep and mindful conversations.

It is not a sales and marketing business.

It's not a human targeting business.

It's a relationship business. Thank goodness.

And it's not that you *can't* have a specialty that arises, or a strong preference that arises, or a niche you declare or create because it inspires you and fits your business plan. Some coaches do that quite well.

It's just that it's not *required* like so many people say it is.

One of the many beauties and benefits of this profession is how creative and unstructured it is. You get to do it your way.

Making the simple complicated is commonplace; making the complicated simple, awesomely simple, that's creativity.

~ Charles Mingus

8.

But on the other hand . . .

A gloriously creative profession like coaching has too much freedom in it to say that there are rules to follow. In the live version of the school, we had a slogan that said, "Tools not rules."

So the seeming rules set down so far—direct conversations instead of marketing . . . open to everyone instead of a niche—are new guidelines that have worked for myself and many others, especially if you're looking for financial strength and prosperity in this profession.

They are thinking tools that are useful for that. Just as when I watch you trying to dig a row in the soil in your garden with your bare hands and I see you're struggling . . . I might bring you a hand trowel so you can see the difference it makes.

That's the spirit in which these experiences and ideas

are being offered here—in the name of getting you clients and leading you onto the path toward prosperity. And just as there are exceptions to rules, there are times when your favorite tools for getting clients can be set aside.

For example, if you are a coach who is doing an online seminar or subscription program, or putting out a new book or audio series, marketing makes good sense. My friend, the great coach Carolyn Freyer-Jones, is putting on a ninety-minute webinar for coaches that over 250 people have registered for. She did that through skillful and content-rich email and social media marketing.

She didn't have a two-hour conversation with all 250 people to bring them to register. That would have taken her months of back-to-back conversations working five days a week for ten hours a day. And that's if everyone she talked to said "yes."

So it's not as if marketing is inappropriate at all times. The lower the fee involved, and the less intimacy and trust are a part of the product or event being offered, the more sense it makes to use marketing and promotion as your tool.

Now on to the idea of having a niche—a special category of client you have special expertise in coaching. Even though, as I've belabored, this is not at all necessary, and none of the really successful coaches I know have an exclusive, restrictive niche they rely on, there are times when a niche can be a good thing.

But most good niches I know of have two qualities:

1. They appeared retroactively, without premeditation.

2. They were not the coach's exclusive category of work.

By retroactively, I mean they were accidental. A coach would coach an aspiring actor who was referred to her by a client who was a talent agent, and after having success with that actor she would start having other actors come to her from referral and word-of-mouth, and the better she got at learning their profession and challenges, the better she got at coaching actors—and the next thing you know, she has a niche.

That kind of accidental niche is a good thing because it helps you get clients in that category through referral and reputation. Coaches I know who get those kinds of niches still have strong practices coaching all other kinds of people and are not restricted to actors.

The main point here is that, contrary to what is being taught to coaches, you don't have to choose ahead of time that you only want to coach actors. If she had done that she may never have found that first actor/client, even though she was wasting all her client-prospecting time looking at that narrow category and all the while making no money and going out of business.

Early in my career I was referred to a company that made aluminum pellets. The owner of the company wanted a coach for his CEO, but the CEO would have to agree to hire me.

The old "rule" of needing to have a niche, or of at least being able to demonstrate the special expertise the niche is supposed to give you up front, was haunting the back of my mind when I had my introductory conversation with the CEO.

I pictured and assumed that the ideal conversation would have gone this way:

CEO: We manufacture and sell aluminum pellets here. Do you know anything about this field?

ME: What, pellets? Aluminum pellets? Are you kidding? Pellets are my passion, especially aluminum pellets. I love them. In fact I keep a bucket of them right here by my desk. Sometimes when I'm procrastinating on something, I just run my fingers through those pellets and they put me right back on track.

CEO: Really?

ME: Oh, yes. And they have to be aluminum. No other pellet works for me. One time someone working in the field of wood pellets was wanting my coaching and I said, "Absolutely not. No offense, but I think wood pellets are on their way out. I work in aluminum and that's it!"

CEO: Wow! You're obviously what we need here. When can we start?

Fortunately that conversation never happened. He did ask me what I knew about metals manufacturing and international sales, and I said, "Absolutely nothing." After a few good, long conversations he realized that I'd be coaching *him*, not the pellets, and anything I needed to know about his industry I would learn along the way.

I worked with him for years thereafter, and he even said later in the relationship that my *lack* of prior knowledge of his industry was an advantage in our work, because his previous industry consultants always arrived with pre-conceived ideas about how that industry should be run (it was their niche), and their sessions were unimaginative and ultimately unhelpful.

Potential clients actually appreciate coaches who show up open and empty, curious and excited about co-creating a future based on infinite possibilities.

Curiosity is
the most powerful force
on this planet.

~ Dr. Zach Bush

9.

Base yourself on infinite possibilities

Your future as a prosperous coach is for you to create. It won't be something that happens to you.

And for it to be created quickly, powerfully and gracefully, you might want to begin by learning (and then integrating) the benefit of creating your future *from* the future, instead of allowing it to be created from the past.

One of the biggest influences in my own transformation from being a **victim** (of other people, events, circumstances, and my belief in my permanent personality—which was dominated by weaknesses, character flaws and fears) to being an **owner** (of my capacity and freedom to create my personality—who I was being in the world—and my future) was Werner Erhard.

It was from him (and his associates who shared his

philosophy through books and seminars) that I learned the difference between a future that was merely a perpetuation of the past, and a future that was, as he said, "created from the future."

A created future holds more possibility than a default future (evolving from inertia . . . the future most people live into).

In his book called *Community: The Structure of Belonging*, Peter Block shares part of a personal correspondence from Werner Erhard, who explained it this way:

> In summary, 1) One gets complete with the past, which takes it out of the future (being complete with the past is not to forget the past);
>
> 2) In the room that is now available in the future when one's being and action are no longer shaped by the past, one creates a future (a future that moves, touches, and inspires one);
>
> 3) That future starts to shape one's being and actions in the present so that they are consistent with realizing that future.

Reading that quickly, it may not hit you with the same amount of bricks that it hit me at the time when my life was at such a turning point.

But even if it hits you with just a little piece of a brick for now, or even just a little brick dust (instead of the ton I got hit with by this), then it was worth sharing with you in the name of moving you into the future you want your coaching practice to thrive in.

And how does this visionary wisdom help me get clients?

(I knew you would ask.)

You don't need a paintbrush to be creative.
Your own unique perspective is your brush.

You don't need an instrument to be creative.
Your body-mind is your instrument.

You don't need a canvas to be creative.
Your friends and family and relationships
are your canvas.

~ Corey W. deVos

10.

You can *create* a
future full of clients

Most people are either stuck in the past or worried about the future. The idea of creating a future from the future they want is new to them.

I'll tell you how it helped me and how, later down the road, it has helped the coaches I've been coaching and teaching throughout all these years.

Creating the future from the future (both for me and my client) means dropping the habit of seeing myself as being created by and made up of my past. Dropping the habit of only being my biographical self.

Almost all potential coaching clients will show up in their first conversations with you as being their biographical self only. Their ego. And that is the very habit that has kept them stuck and challenged.

If you can help them with that, and release them from that unnecessary straitjacket, you will be worth all the coaching money they can pay you.

The more that straitjacket is loosened and even cut away in little pieces during your first intake or enrollment conversations, the more likely they will want to continue talking to you, this time in an upleveled, committed and paid professional program of coaching.

How can you verify that they are creating their lives from their past and not their future . . . that they are living as their biographical selves?

You can tell by the way they talk:

"I have a pattern of . . ."

"I'm not one who . . ."

"I'm hardwired that way . . ."

"That's not the way I am . . ."

"I always . . ."

"I never . . ."

"My biggest fear is . . ."

"It's not in my nature to . . ."

That is their fixed, permanent, biographical self talking to you. That self has taken all its past decisions, behaviors, and feelings and melted them into a solid identity. They have confused what I have done with who I am.

I was at a Byron Katie seminar once when I heard her

say something I never forgot. She said, "Do you know what I love most about the past? It's over!"

Your life doesn't have to be a tale told by an idiot. Stop putting your past into your future—you will have way more space to create. And you just might notice you have more freedom today.

~ Trevor Timbeck

11.

Habits disguise themselves as traits and characteristics

All of these qualities, traits, labels, character flaws and personal weaknesses you and I and your potential clients talk about are not the result of who we are.

They're not qualities emanating from some permanent identity. They don't come from that at all.

They come from repetition. Actually they come from habit, but habit comes from repetition.

So any "negative personal characteristic" your potential client presents to you (or which you see in yourself) is only a habit misunderstood as a characteristic. It's a description of repetition, not of who we are. And what you, the coach, love most about negative repetition is that it's not permanent. Even though your potential client thinks it is.

This discussion right here, about how changeable people are, about how changeable personalities are, about how possible it is to change who you are being and thereby what you are doing, is the primary discussion, however long it takes to unfurl, that converts a potential client into a client.

If you want it to be, the old, habitual version of "you" is over. Of all the possibilities a prospective client sees during their first conversations with a coach, this one is by far the most exciting.

You are not the limited person you think you are. Any trained Buddhist teacher can tell you with all the conviction of personal experience that, really, you're the very heart of compassion, completely aware, and fully capable of achieving the greatest good, not only for yourself, but for everyone and everything that you can imagine.

~ **Mingyur Rinpoche**

12.

Imagine no more failed sales calls

Just a quick review:

Clients don't come from being advertised to.

Clients come from conversations.

And once you wake up to that realization and shift your time and attention from self-promotion to conversations, your life gets better, as does your bank account.

This is the fundamental shift that runs through every idea in this book. It's a shift that (once it starts to get practiced) works better and better as you go, and feels better the more comfortable and conditioned you are to doing it. And like a diamond, it has many facets.

Such as the shift in mindset from sales to service. A day spent serving others feels much more rewarding than a day of failed sales efforts.

A day spent creating relationships is much more productive and fulfilling than a day filled with marketing frustration and sales rejection. In this system you will spend your practice-building time in cultivation and creation instead of frustrating promotion, persuasion and manipulation.

There is even a spiritual facet to this basic shift. You are shifting away from the ego and its painful self-consciousness into the much more peaceful and expansive world of compassion, understanding and service.

By shifting to this brand new operating principle throughout your day, client cultivation becomes something that you look forward to, instead of always feeling like it's "the hard part" of your coaching life.

Once I saw this, and verified its effectiveness, little by little I began to fall in love with the very thing I used to dread and avoid: client cultivation.

And people tend to get really good at what they love doing.

One of the best ways to get clients is to stop failing at it. One of the most successful activities we have taught in the coaching school is to create a "Not Yet" file. Every "no" becomes a "not yet."

If I have a conversation or two with you and you choose not to hire me as your coach, I can process that as my having failed, or I can see the deeper and truer reality that I have just created a relationship. I will put your name and my notes on our talks in my "Not Yet" file. Some day in the future I will check back in with you to see how it's going in your world.

I can't tell you how many clients over the years have come from my "Not Yet" file.

These are people who know there was no sales pitch. They know that when we talked, a relationship was created. They were not reluctant to reach out to me after the talks because they didn't sense disappointment from me. They didn't pick up on any hard feelings. The door felt open.

In the past, before I learned to create each "no" as a "not yet," people felt my cold and immediate loss of interest in who they were and what they were doing. Although I never said it out loud, people could feel my thoughts: "If you're not going to pay me, you're dead to me. Thanks a lot for wasting my time!"

Those thoughts come from a world of sales, persuasion and attempted manipulation. No one enjoys that world. Not the coach and not the potential client.

You don't have to go there. Let's look at some better places you can go.

Choosing to create enjoyment
instead of solely creating results
will bring you both.

~ **Jason Goldberg**

13.

I couldn't deal with "rejection"

B ack in my early years as a coach I processed "no" as rejection.

I would take it personally. If you said "no" to coaching with me I would make up a story that you thought time spent with me wasn't worth paying for. I'd sink down in my chair and think, "Apparently I'm not worth it."

In some of my early sessions with my coach I would tell him I was having a hard time with all the rejection.

ME: How do you deal with the rejection that comes with this profession?

MY COACH: I don't deal with rejection because there isn't any.

ME: No rejection? Everybody says "yes" to working with you?

COACH: No, of course not. But why is that rejection? That's not rejection at all. That's only information. What the "no" tells me is that she or he will not be working with me right now. If I spend my time creating a story of rejection and then another story about having to work with my feelings that arise from that story, I am missing the opportunity to connect with someone new.

ME: It sure feels like rejection to me. I feel like I'm back in high school when I couldn't get a date for the prom and started considering suicide.

COACH: You couldn't get a date, is that true?

ME: So we're going to do Byron Katie work now?

COACH: No, it's just a question. We're trying to get to what's real and true.

ME: People didn't want to go with me.

COACH: How many did you ask?

ME: One . . . or two . . . I asked two.

COACH: Two! Out of hundreds? And your conclusion was that you couldn't get a date? The math of that is faulty. Your experiment was flawed . . . your sample size was much too small.

ME: I see that now.

COACH: But you're doing it again in your coaching practice.

Coaching sessions like that are hard to forget. Sometimes the insights I get from them take a while to permeate the entire human operating system.

Sometimes my stories that arise from past conditioning and thought habits take time to fade away. But the insight doesn't fade. And as the clouding and veiling stories move out, the light of insight grows brighter and more helpful every day.

I heard a colleague on a group call answer a new coach's question in an unusual way. The new coach asked him, "What do you do when you have run out of people to talk to?"

He answered, "There are eight billion people on this planet and they all want their lives to change for the better. I assume you've been through them all?"

People think I'm disciplined.

It is not discipline. It is devotion.

There is a great difference.

~ **Luciano Pavarotti**

14.

Where should my attention be today?

Imagine there is a light within you. Picture it shining from your heart . . . or from your mind, if that works better. See it as a magic beam that causes anything it shines on to grow. And before you dismiss this exercise as some kind of new age hallucination, note that it is the *most practical advice* I've ever received or given when it comes to creating anything, including clients.

That beam of light is nothing more than your time and attention. Where is it being consciously directed during your work day?

What you shine it on will grow.

If it's being directed at the cultivation of clients, your client list will grow. If it's being directed at playing your piano, your piano playing skills will grow. If it's being directed at your garden out back, your garden will grow, inch by inch, row by row.

Time and attention! Practical. Proven. Measurable!

As long as we remember it is there, always. And it is powerful. I spent many lost years forgetting it was there. My time and attention were whirling, sprocketing and shooting out everywhere like an out of control fire hose spinning wildly on the ground.

Some coaches call it "shiny object syndrome." Those attention grabbers. They distract me from my path.

We really do "know" the difference between a shiny object and pure gold. But just knowing isn't enough. To get clients we have to practice giving our time and attention to the communication and service that leads to getting clients.

If a coach asks me "How do I get more clients?" my short (but accurate) answer is always, "Give the relationship-building process more time and attention."

Learning to mindfully focus on what I really want takes practice. Just like playing darts, or shooting a bow and arrow, it takes practice. In coaching, it's target practice. And it requires knowing what and where the target is.

And why can't it be fun? Why does it have to be a grind that requires fierce, inborn discipline? Why not make the practice itself fun, just like throwing darts?

I used to hold my happiness hostage until I reached some future big financial outcome. But as I worked with my own coach and other coaches I found that I could be happy now—during the practice—and not wait until the practice delivered what I wanted. The more I did that, the more I looked forward to and devoted myself to the practice, the faster the intended outcomes would arrive.

It's never too late to be
what you might have been.

~ **George Eliot**

15.

Willing to revisit priorities

You have priorities, right? The activities that are most important to you are your highest priorities, and the ones that are least important are the lowest.

And because, as a coach, you don't have a boss or supervisor looking over your shoulder all day making sure you are prioritizing what the organizational mission needs from you, it's up to you to take on that leadership role yourself—to consciously and deliberately prioritize what's important.

Like getting clients.

You can consciously prioritize this activity.

Most coaches actually subconsciously de-prioritize getting clients because it can feel hard and awkward, especially if they are in their social self instead of their professional self. The social self is pure ego, taking everything personally, trying to make an impression, worried about "how I'm coming across" to people or always being insecure about "whether I'm bothering them."

But what makes the social self—with all its awkwardness and de-prioritizing (and procrastination and discouragement)—go away?

Time and attention—given to my professional mission and goals. The more of that you give to anything the less awkward it feels. Soon it becomes free and easy.

I didn't know this at the start of my coaching career. Although if you had told me this wisdom, it might have made good sense intellectually. Up there on the level of information . . . philosophy I approve of on the level of logic and thinking. But it would never have dropped into the level of transformation. I was like most coaches I knew back then, always adding more and more information about coaching, but not ever staying with it long enough for it to become transformation.

My priorities each day, back then, were like cockroaches that scattered the minute the light was turned on. They ran all over, trying to hide behind my money fears and social-self insecurity.

I'd be on the internet frantically searching all around for what other coaches were saying and doing. I'd look for hope and motivation in YouTubes. I'd watch TED Talks about making big dreams come true, then I'd check my email again, check the news sites to see if we still had a world, then grab my open paperback on the desk about "meridian tapping for abundance," then I'd step up and tap between my shoulder blades and between my forefinger and thumb, then check my online bank account, then I'd think one should never try to sell and advertise on an empty stomach so I'd run down to the kitchen to fry a couple eggs, then back upstairs to the computer to see if I could write a blog post but find that after a couple tries my medical condition called "writer's block" would kick in, and after standing back up to do some kundalini fire breathing for energy it would occur to me that the substance I needed to jump into the activity of getting clients with proper mental clarity was coffee.

As I'd stand over the coffee machine, waiting for it to finish heating up my brew, I would hear my wife in the other room asking me how it was going, and I'd lie and say it was going great and that I was just taking a badly needed break from "work."

After she asked another question I'd stroll into her office, cup in hand and sit down on the sofa for a nice long chat. I'd tell myself that good personal relationships in any kind of family require compassionate listening, so I'd ask her about her day. She'd say it was fine but she hadn't fed the dogs yet. So I'd say, "Let me feed them!" And she'd ask if I had time for that, and I'd say, "Oh yeah, I'm on my break, I'll do it!"

After feeding the dogs I'd see the piano over there in the corner of the room and ask her if it would bother her if I played a little bit before going back upstairs to work.

I'd say, "I find that music lifts my spirits!" as I started playing "Everybody Hurts," the first of many sad songs. After a while I'd shout out to her, "OMG, I got carried away! Time to get back to work!"

Then back upstairs in my office I'd check my emails for a while before jumping on Facebook, where I'd spend half an hour (at least) seeing who "liked" or even "loved" any of the posts I'd been making. A quick glance at the clock showed me it was now time for lunch, after which I'd be going to the gym, because it's pretty hard to build a prosperous coaching practice if you let yourself go physically and don't build strength to get your self-esteem up.

I had no respect for the power of creatively-chosen priorities. Priorities! I couldn't understand their value. And that if they aren't mindfully chosen and attended to, emotional anarchy sets in. You wonder what you're doing wrong. Other people who don't coach as well as you do, who haven't been trained as well as you have, are getting clients, and you're not. It doesn't seem fair.

But what you are doing wrong is simple. It's merely a blindness to the creative power of time and attention. Your time and attention are simply not going into what you most want to create. You're throwing your darts all over the bar. People are spilling their drinks and running for cover. The bouncer has been summoned.

The beauty of practice is that it transforms us
so that we outgrow our original intentions
—and keep going!

Our motivations for practicing evolve
as we mature.

~ Ken Wilber

16.

Show me your calendar!

And if you are in England, this means, "Show me your diary!"

Either way, I mean actually show it to me. Pass it on over so I can look at it. (When I'm sitting with someone who wants my coaching on how to get clients, I often actually do this.)

Why do I want to look at your calendar? Because it's going to show me your priorities. It will show me what you are committed to actually having happen. It shows me where your time and attention are going.

You can do this for yourself right now. Get your calendar out, pretend you are coaching (or leading or managing) yourself, and take a look. What's there? What's written down?

Most people's calendars only list appointments, in

person or by phone or video, with doctors, lawyers, friends, personal trainers, yoga sessions, and pre-existing client sessions.

So the first thing we are searching the calendar for are appointments for conversations with prospective clients. How many were there last week? The week before?

If we don't find many, we are waking up to one big, important reason why we are not getting clients. Clients come from conversations. (Although most people believe clients must come from self-promotion, marketing, personal branding and getting one's name "out there.")

But clients actually come from conversations. Relationships. Mutual explorations of possibility. And this is what soon becomes the fun part of your day at work as a coach.

This is the real secret of life—to be completely engaged with what you are doing in the here and now. And instead of calling it work, realize it is play.

~ **Alan Watts**

17.

Commitment to client cultivation

The second thing we are looking for are dedicated blocks of time that we actually *see on the calendar* for client cultivation.

This time is *set aside for* exploring, investigating, connecting and inviting people into those conversations.

Your calendar tells us what you are actually committed to. And that's good news, because that commitment is yours to change and create so that it *consciously and intentionally* leads you to getting clients

Many coaches I know and work with make the mistake of confusing commitment with intention. They think they're the same thing. And by thinking that, by living in that misunderstanding, they lose all the power commitment has.

Meredith was a fairly new coach who kept telling me she didn't keep her commitments.

"I committed to making $80,000 last year," she'd say, "but unfortunately I didn't keep that commitment."

I told her that, therefore, it wasn't a commitment. It was an intention.

"Why wasn't it a commitment? For most of last year I was really committed to it."

I told her the way I knew it wasn't a commitment was that it didn't happen. Therefore it was an intention.

"So commitments have to actually happen?"

Yes. Commitments are for things you know you can make happen. You can commit to a process but not to an outcome. I can commit to putting ten or even twenty hours a week into communication with prospective clients. I can put blocks in my calendar for client cultivation: finding and talking to potential clients or people who can lead me to potential clients.

I then track my hours.

A commitment is a solemn promise I make to myself. I'm going to DO THIS, and I can count on it, you can count on it and the universe can count on it.

If I have a goal or intention to win a medal in the (senior) Olympics marathon race, I can and will commit to my schedule of training runs. But saying I'm "committed" to winning that medal is a misuse of the word. I have every *intention* of winning the medal. And that goal can serve me by inspiring me to keep my training commitment, but I can't commit to an outcome I can't ultimately control.

I can commit to the *process* that I believe will give me the best chance of reaching my goal.

To get clients, I will get the best guidance I can from a coach or a group of coaches I've joined on what process I should practice that has the best track record for getting clients. A good coach will tailor their recommended process to people I already know, how I like to communicate, what I've already done in life and what my skill level is as a coach.

Now I can either commit to practicing that process or not. Most coaches begin with an *intention* to follow that process, which means it's kind of floating around in the back of their minds to do it. Some days they do it, some days they don't. That's clearly what was happening in Meredith's relationship with her $80,000 goal last year.

But once she becomes more devoted to creating a successful practice she can use commitment as the true superpower it is. Once she has looked long enough at her calendar to see that the most important factor in the mission of getting clients has only been showing up there infrequently, she can take the next step: actually booking immovable, committed time for pre-conversation exploration and cultivation.

Most people know that it can take a while to get a potential client interested in having a good, long, scheduled conversation. But they also know, theoretically and intellectually, that it's a vital part of the process. Without it, there won't be conversations. (And without conversations, there won't be clients.)

And, in the past how much definite, unmovable time has been calendarized and committed to this activity? Almost always the answer is none. It lived only as an intention.

"I try to get to it when I can," is the usual answer. "I know I need to try to remember to do more of it. I know it's important. Now that you bring it up, I can see that it's important. It might even be the missing piece in the whole puzzle for me. I don't know why I don't remember to do more of it."

I'll tell you why. It hasn't been scheduled. Time has not been set aside for it. I don't see it in your calendar. That's not an opportunity for self-criticism, guilt or shame. That's a revelation. It's a moment of enlightenment, and quite often the turning point in your coaching practice.

The moment it goes from financial struggle to prosperity.

And once the storm is over, you won't remember how you made it through, how you managed to survive. You won't even be sure, whether the storm is really over. But one thing is certain. When you come out of the storm, you won't be the same person who walked in. That's what this storm's all about.

~ Haruki Murakami
Kafka on the Shore

18.

Blooming and flourishing as a coach

I do a teaching segment in the coaching prosperity school called "Tree of Life." It's about growth and flourishing as a committed path, not just an ideal scene.

The first few years of our lives (and here I am drawing a tree on the whiteboard to represent your life, and pointing to the lowest part of the tree), from zero to three or four years old or so, we are powered by our **Want To**. We are little children wanting what we want because we want it! We roam the world asking for what we want and not being afraid to ask for it again and again, whatever the first answer is!

As we get higher up into the middle of the tree we are growing older, interacting with society now, so we switch from **Want To** to **Should Do**, trying to find out from others what they think we should do . . . trying to fit in, trying to get approval.

Most people *never leave* that stage. It becomes a life of pleasing rather than serving, a life of reacting rather than creating, and hoping to settle in safely somewhere rather than progressing and growing. That's the dull and thick middle trunk of the tree I point to.

What should I do? How should I do it? Who should I appear to be? Who should I talk to? What should I talk about?

Limitation folds into further limitation.

However!!! Not everyone stays stuck on "should." Have you noticed? Some unusual people just seem to keep going. They keep ascending. They don't stop at "I guess I've arrived" in dull, disappointed, safe adulthood.

Somehow they pass through the **Should** stage and just keep going! How does that happen?

Maybe, for some, it's through Divine intervention. They receive a jolt of awakening or enlightenment to the creative energy at the heart of who they are, and their thought-based limitations fall away.

Or maybe it happens through coaching, and especially through being coached. That's where it happened for me and for so many of the people I've worked with.

Through coaching we can re-connect to the **Want To**

we were born with and create a life from what we love creating—that part of the tree up at the top, the part that has all the fruit, all the flowers . . . all the true flourishing.

So when you talk to a prospective client, your job is not to be impressive, sound wise, and persuade them that coaching is worth paying for.

Your job is to find out what they want. Then you re-connect them to *their* **Want To**. The same one they had as kids. It's in there. It has to feel safe to come out, and that's what starts to happen, that safety . . . that possibility . . . when you are in your first conversations, before they are an official client.

That's a big part of what has them say "Yes!" to working with you.

It's not the problem that causes our suffering;
it's our thinking about the problem.

~ **Byron Katie**

19.

Is there a right way to get clients?

We've talked about a lot of the wrong ways. But as long as you become aware of and are willing to practice the basic principles of serving before selling, listening before talking, giving before getting and directly connecting versus massively marketing, you'll be glad to see that when you're inside that guidance system you don't need to always figure out the right way.

Over time, it simply becomes *your* way.

When I wrote a book about creativity (*Creator*) I wanted to share what was, for me, the most important element in creating anything.

I called it "the path."

A friend recently asked me for help. She said, "I find myself switching back and forth between things and not really creating. Once I hit a snag I am tempted to stop or switch to something else. How did you solve this?"

I thought for a long time. Then it hit me. This isn't about some personal problem that has to be solved. It's more about a direction. In other words:

There is a path.

A path to the completion of what I want to create.

A new song? A freshly painted bedroom? The ability to play *Over the Rainbow* on the ukulele?

The creation of a prosperous coaching business?

Whatever I want to create!

There is a path.

And when I'm not on that path, I'm not creating.

And when I *am* on the path, I'm creating.

Sometimes I hit a snag and am tempted to leave the path for a while. Sometimes I do leave, and walk along a side road.

But the path is always there. It waits for me. It has no judgment. It will wait years for me.

My friend asked, "How did you solve this?"

There was nothing to solve. Because there was no real problem. There was only but always a path. And the good news is that a path is not a problem.

It's something you're on or you're not.

If I see that I've left the path for too long to do

something else, I go back to the path. If I want to create what the path leads to, I know to go back to the path.

One new perception, one fresh thought, one act of surrender, one change of heart, one leap of faith, can change your life forever.

~ **Robert Holden**

20.

What if people DO want coaching?

Once we've awakened to the fact that most people don't want coaching—they just want their problems solved, their challenges met, and their possibilities realized—we can remember to talk to prospective clients about those things, not coaching.

But there are exceptions to this guideline, and they are good for the building of your prosperous practice.

For example, if another coach approaches you, and she already knows the value and power of coaching because she does it all day, and she sees you as a coach who is more experienced than she is, a coach who might help her get closer to where you are, then yes, talk about coaching.

Why? Because it's what she wants!

There's another time, too.

As you get to know the prospective client you're exploring with, they might begin to warm up to the whole idea and want to know more about coaching.

Our first impulse is to be impressive on the subject . . . talk about our training or certification and our client success stories or the impressive companies or people who have hired us, etc. Very impressive!!

But the real gold is in sharing how you yourself have been coached. What it's done for you. How hopeless you felt about certain things prior to coaching. People listen differently to that than they do to someone crowing about credentials and achievements.

So learn to share your own personal experiences. Show them the "before and after" pictures of your heart and soul.

I've written multiple stories in my previous books about what coaching has done for me. My changes from victim to owner, from pessimist to optimist, from reactor to creator. These transformations were huge and life-changing. And potential clients are much more interested in hearing these real life experiences from the one who experienced them than they are in hearing claims and promises.

They'd rather hear how my life has changed than how hard I've tried to hype my business.

And as interesting and inspiring as these personal

stories can be, I always want to return quickly to the prospect's world in that conversation. What would they like to have shifted and changed?

The reason most coaches don't talk about being coached is because they are stuck in a myth. They believe they have to appear to be superior in every way to the other person in the conversation. They think, "I don't want them to think I need coaching. I want to come across as someone who has their act together. Someone superior to them! Because if I'm not superior, why would they hire me?"

I used to try to look skilled and educated and worth a lot of money in my conversations with people considering coaching. I thought I had to radiate wisdom and superiority if I was to even get a second conversation with my potential client.

It took a good while . . . a good, impoverished while . . . before I finally saw clearly that my previous imperfections did more to build trust than my previous achievements did.

If you help others, you will be helped. Perhaps tomorrow, perhaps in a hundred years, but you will be helped. Nature must pay off the debt. It is a mathematical law and all life is mathematical.

~ **Gurdjieff**

21.

Curiosity is the ultimate power

Before that next conversation with a prospective client, jot down questions you want to ask that person. Visit their website and social media posts and let your curiosity grow. Read their blogs. Go deep.

Because there is no initial relationship-builder that connects more deeply and intensely than curiosity.

When you first talk with someone, stay open, stay compassionate and stay curious.

Consistent curiosity demonstrates to the other person that you are more interested in understanding them than you are in having them understand you and your greatness. Most coaches talk too much when they are in first conversations with a prospective client.

I was no exception to that. I was so insecure about whether I was qualified as a coach that I talked my head off trying to convince them of my value. Had I been more curious and more interested they would have had a direct experience of my value.

Back then I am sure most people I was talking to heard this: "No, really I'm real! No, really, I can do this, I can coach you. Let me tell you more and more about ME! And after I've exhausted that subject let me move on to what I have DONE! After that, we'll talk about what I think can do for YOU, and then we'll get on to why I am worth every penny of my fee! I'm certified! I'm justified! I'm qualified! I'm verified! I'm sanctified! Look over here, eyes right here, so you can savor your good fortune: I am me!"

Not in those exact words of course, but I'm sure my prospective client felt that that was the message.

Sometimes coaches tell me that they have had a really great and "super powerful!" sample session and that their prospect even sent them an email afterward about how impressive and powerful the coach was in that conversation—only to finish the email by saying "But I'm going to pass for now."

The coach says to me, "WTF? If it was so powerful, if I was so powerful, why are they passing?"

I might say, "Tell me what you know about them?"

"What do you mean?"

"What do they want? What's their biggest fear? How

would they want their life to change? What have they tried so far to make the change? What are their limiting beliefs that showed themselves in the conversation?"

The coach usually says, "Oh. Um. I'm not sure."

And I would remind that coach that this whole thing called coaching is not about your credentials or your opinions. It's about change. In the other person. And if you could leave your ego—which is to say your insecurity—out of the equation, you'd be getting clients more easily.

Remember that the final decision to use your services will always occur in their world, not yours. So even when they ask about you, keep it brief and to the point, but return immediately to curiosity.

Curiosity is love and caring in action. It is experiential proof to your prospective client of your commitment to understand them, to see their challenges clearly, in an optimistic non-judgmental way.

The more passionate curiosity you demonstrate, the more the potential client will want to keep talking to you.

Again: Every sale of services takes place in the other person's world, not your own. That's where the decision is made to hire you and pay a good fee. Not in your world, but theirs. So stay in their world! Keep coming back to it.

The only way to really get into a prospective client's world is to continuously ask genuinely curious questions and follow up questions. Don't talk about yourself until invited to. And even then, tell a short case history story about a client you helped, or about how coaching helped you . . . but have that story be related to what your prospect wants. Then finish that story with another question to them so you quickly get back into their world. You don't want to remain in your world, tempting as that may be.

The appeal of your services always shows up in their world, not yours. Your ego won't see this. It will keep trying to be impressive. But you will soon wake up to the fact that attempts to be impressive work against your chances of getting this person as a client.

I was like a lot of newer coaches who come into our school. I was always trying to establish superiority over the other person. It was my ego taking over the conversation. I was operating from the vague, somewhat hidden and devastating belief that to get a client I had to make a great and powerful impression. I wasn't realizing that the kind of impression I was making would be described at a crime scene as "blunt force trauma."

But as I learned over the years, my trying to establish superiority over someone else does not bring us together. It drives us apart. There is no developing feeling of relatedness. There is no experience of non-judgmental understanding or empathy. The connection is lost. The other person, experiencing so much ego activity, retreats into their own armored ego. My primary goal should be to create a sense of safety, but in the early days I was creating the opposite. The prospective client would then drop into self-defense. They'd then tell me they didn't really have major problems, just a few minor ones. So I never found out what they really wanted. It didn't feel safe for them to share that with me. They didn't think I'd understand because they didn't experience any valid attempts on my side of the conversation to understand them. And, therefore, why pay a large fee to solve small, inconsequential problems? It doesn't make sense.

Sometimes I will assign a coach the homework of watching Sherlock Holmes. Even if they think watching Tony Robbins or Marianne Williamson videos makes more sense so they can learn to speak more powerfully about all the motivational and spiritual breakthroughs they can offer a client.

Sherlock is all about curiosity. Curiosity is the most powerful relationship-creator in the world. It is an amazing mix of love and genius. Compassion and intelligence. Commitment to understand and assist the other person.

Instead of commitment to sell the other person something.

Curiosity versus manipulation is love versus fear.

Look back to when you were first dating, courting and falling in love. You became fascinated by the other person. All your loving questions!

"What's your favorite color?"

"Royal blue."

"Blue?? Wow that's amazing to me! You are so upbeat and positive I would have thought some variation on red, or maybe bright pink or dusty rose."

"No, it's blue. I've always loved it. My grandmother gave me a blue bicycle when I was little."

"What . . . wait . . . your grandmother? You haven't told me about your grandmother! What was she like?"

This is curiosity, and this is love. Love is what it is, and curiosity is how it is expressed.

Curiosity is what is expressed, and love is what is felt.

If this couple marries and later begins piling up resentments, "unmet needs," and all kinds of stories about each other over the years, they may think they have "fallen out of love," and in a last ditch effort to save the marriage go to counseling—where the counselor asks if you even know your partner's favorite color. You think for a while and say, "I think it's green." But your partner knows it's blue and remembers when you knew that too. Back when you were "in love," which is to say, back when you were curious. Same thing.

Also, you can think back to those early months when you told your friends how fascinated and attracted you were to your new love because of all the curious and intriguing ways in which you two were different. You might have said, "Boy, it's really true that opposites attract!"

Those very differences you loved at the curious beginning are now being described by your divorce attorney as "irreconcilable differences."

Curiosity is not only love in action, but a demonstration of your commitment to understand and uncover the glorious complexity of the other person's network of beliefs and experiences. You are like Sherlock: the more curious you are, the faster we will solve things.

When the connectivity of curiosity is not there it will always feel as if you are looking down on the other person. Dismissive of their inner world. Too ready to give your standard one-size-fits-all advice and assignments.

I used to be that way as a coach until I gradually and almost reluctantly woke up to what I was doing and who I was being. My lack of curiosity looked like I didn't care about them. "Hey, my coaching helps everyone! I don't have to know about you, I'll solve whatever you give me. Like my business card says: Superior wisdom for inferior people. I'm the Answer Man, so why would I focus on questions?"

Overheard recently from another room in the house as a Hallmark movie that was playing:

"Why did you leave Bradford for that young . . . farmer?"

"Because . . . he gets me."

You alone can do it,
but you cannot do it alone.

~ O. Hobart Mowrer

22.

Give them CONTENT, not concept!

When people were interested in the ACS (the LIVE Coaching Prosperity School, also known as Advanced Client Systems) we sent **content** from the course to them: audios and videos and sometimes even books that delivered the **content** of the course—the actual teachings and systems that would occur in the course.

Even the so-called "Sales Page" for the ACS gave away the ten big ideas they would learn in the school. When people were still undecided, we sent more stuff. In the early days, before the ACS became so popular via word-of-mouth that it practically filled on its own, I would often work for hours with a potential attendee, delivering the content from the course to her right then and there.

When people receive valuable content from a group or

event they are considering attending, they have an opportunity to experience directly whether the content is useful to them. When that person only hears concepts, which show up as promised features and benefits, they don't have anything other than blind faith to base their decision on. They hear about features: live meetings! guest speakers! Zoom webinars! daily email Q&A! video tips! books and audios! etc. And they hear benefits: "YOU WILL learn to get clients! Learn to build your practice through serving, not selling! Connect with other coaches! Find out what prosperous coaches do to build their practices! Eliminate your money fears!"

Those are all empty concepts—thoughts and pictures in the client's head that they have no way of knowing whether to believe. And it's not that the group leader trying to sell the group or event is being dishonest. All the features and benefits can be honest and real descriptions of what occurs and what people get. But how does the prospect ever know?

Even in individual, one-on-one coaching I see a lot of coaches' websites that pump up the concepts of coaching: "Find your core value!" "Live the life you dream!" "Develop a purpose!" "Connect better with others!" "Achieve more work-life balance!" "Be all you can be!" "Create your legacy!"

But those are all concepts, which means they are empty and ineffective when it comes to helping someone decide whether to work with you.

But when you give a prospective client the *experience* of working with you . . . when they can feel the actual CHANGE occur in their life when they spend time sharing their challenges with you . . . they now have received the CONTENT of what your coaching does. And because they have experienced it, it's nothing they have to conceptualize.

Give it a whirl! Experiment before you agree or disagree.

Experiments never fail.

~ Dale Dauten

23.

Remember who you really are

When coaches seek to get their first clients, they often get confused about what this coaching thing is all about. I have a simple way of describing it to myself: it's coaching.

And the way my service is going to be delivered once the person signs up with me is mine to create. That's one of the many beauties of this profession . . . policy is mine to create. Not theirs.

It took me a good while to understand this simple point: this offer I'm making is for coaching. It's not anything else.

It's not psychiatric care, or a suicide hotline, or domestic violence counseling, or forensic psychology, or treatment for unusual addictions such as eating dirt or other non-edible items.

I'm not making fun of those service categories because

they have their useful place in society. But unless I am professionally trained and certified in those professions, they are not me.

Some newer coaches don't stay strong in their respect and honor for the dignity and honor of this profession. (What other profession has the power to transform lives forever?) The moment they get a client or a prospect, they surrender their leadership and turn the whole process over to the emotional whims of the client no matter how inconsiderate they are. In our school we call that "role reversal."

And the leader of the process sets the policy.

Some coaches make themselves "available" to clients between sessions and some do not. Your coaching practice policy on this is yours to create.

At the beginning, I let this go out of control.

As far as my policies went, I created nothing. I let the world come to me any way it wanted to, thinking that made me look non-judgmental and spiritual, like a Zen monk with a huge heart.

The result? Some clients texted me day and night. Some had people pull me out of meetings I was in at a corporation. So they could talk about their feelings.

One client showed up to a girls' softball game I was watching with questions for me. One sent me daily poems based on dreams she'd had the night before, hoping it would help me understand the "journey" she was on.

I finally woke up to the realization that this profession is fairly new and has no pre-existing rules and regulations that I could learn to follow. At that time, I wished it did! I didn't want to develop my own professional policies or take a "grown-up" kind of responsibility for my own coaching practice, given that I was only in my forties and wasn't really ready to plunge recklessly into adulthood. Not until adulthood and maturity felt authentic. (It could be a long wait!)

But when it reached the breaking point, and it was now a necessity to create my own policies, doing so turned out to be a good thing for me. It strengthened my own professional self-respect and gave clients more reassurance that they were part of an orderly process.

Today my clients can email me between calls and get a short spot call of fifteen minutes if something important comes up between sessions. But I mean "important!"

Not this: "I was cat-napping and an angelic voice whispered for me to contact you. I don't have any idea what it's about? Can we explore? Call me."

You can see why I now want to get an agreement ahead of time, that this between-session availability isn't for every little thing, but only for something that feels too important and urgent to save for the next session.

Most of my clients respect this, but when I do get a client who has never seen a border they wouldn't cross, I'll call a time out and realign with them.

In the long run, clients are better served when they learn to bring their challenges to our pre-scheduled full session because we'll have time to really explore. Sometimes they might have created those challenges for themselves (!) and not realized it. They might want a spot session to talk about how to communicate with their wife when she is angry, shouting and judgmental.

CLIENT: I need 15 minutes.

ME: What's up? Anything we can't save for our session tomorrow?

CLIENT: I don't think so...just need some ideas from you on what to say to my wife...you know, some languaging ideas.

ME: Okay, what's she upset about?

CLIENT: She disagrees with a business decision I made about our company's leadership summit in Hawaii. Which is not her business even.

ME: What was the business decision?

CLIENT: I decided to take my ex-girlfriend along with me on the trip to help me brainstorm some ideas on product innovation for a presentation I have to make. She's good at that. She used to work at Google. Innovation is her zone of genius! When I told my wife about it, she shouted that Brandi was too young to have a zone of genius. "And she's a flirt!" How can I deal with that level of ignorance from my wife? What should I say?

This conversation is an actual spot-coaching session I had not long ago. Can you see where this situation might require more than fifteen minutes to resolve and learn anything from?

Is it probable that fifteen minutes was too short to explore the radical possibility that my client might be creating his own problems in life, and to then show him that if he can create problems he can create the opposite of that, but he has to be willing to see himself as a creator? I'm not good enough to have all that happen in fifteen minutes.

Coaching and conversations with prospects work best

in full sessions, when they can be done in a way that's relaxed and in depth for both people, rather than you and me doing little quick and shallow fixes along the way even if it makes you think you're being more supported by me.

I want clients to appreciate that our best work is often the work we do on the beliefs that may be behind their problems (what's really creating the problems), instead of just giving all power to the problem itself. And to look for some "languaging" to get temporary relief.

And to do that well, we have to have a full session available to us. Because that's coaching. If clients are wanting me to be constantly available for ongoing "support" they will be training themselves, with my help, to think they need constant support. To even live.

Effective coaching doesn't come from "How can I support you?" in every little thing, because it will end up being, "How can I increase your dependency on me?"

Don't set up your practice that way, unless your mission statement is to create a coaching practice devoid of transformation.

I won't judge you for that, because that's what I did at the beginning. I do not want to do it now. I need to remember that I am a coach, not an emotional support animal.

My goal, instead, is to coach in a deeply transformative

way so that the client can eventually stand up on their own, without ongoing support. Stand strong. Stand tall. Focused on who you are being, not every little thing you're doing.

Support has a place in a coaching relationship, when it's appropriate and not central to the relationship. But here is a good description of what I don't want to be:

"Federal regulations allow a legitimate emotional support animal, whether it be a dog, a cat, a pot-bellied pig or even a miniature horse in one case, to travel on airplanes in the cabin with the owner, outside of a carrier, and for free if the owner has proper documentation, which means a letter from a doctor."

And the day came when the risk it took to remain tight inside the bud was more painful than the risk it took to blossom.

~ Anaïs Nin

24.

People want to help you get clients

In the *Divine Comedy*, Dante is trying to make his way out of Hell and he asks his guide, Virgil, how they can get out of the terrible situation facing them.

Virgil says, "The way out is through."

The poet Robert Frost also wrote that "the best way out is through."

Dante was talking about Hell, and Frost was talking about the woods.

An old gospel song applies this wisdom a different way, singing: "My heaven is so high you can't get over it, so low you can't go under it, so wide you can't get around it . . . you gotta come in at the door."

Coaches looking for new clients are almost always looking for ways to go over, under or around the people they already know to find new prospects. They try to connect with people who not only don't know them, but who don't even understand what "coaching" really is.

Is it like therapy? Or like business consulting? Or what? And why would I need it? And who are you again?

That was never a conversation I looked forward to. It made me feel like I was bothering people. No wonder I procrastinated on that unpleasant activity, even though I thought that was what I had to do to get clients.

When I learned that this thing called "how to get clients" could be kinder, gentler, friendlier and more fun (not to mention more effective), my world turned right-side up. My bank account was no longer being written by Stephen King.

I learned that the best way out of the woods was through. And that to reach the heaven of a prosperous professional life I had to come in at the door.

What was that door? It was relationships. Relationships I already had. People who were happy to take my calls, answer my messages and emails. People I enjoyed communicating with.

I asked for time with my accountant. I wanted to tell him about my business. He was happy to see me. When he understood what coaching really was, and how it could help people find more success in the inner world as well as in their careers, I told him I'd give him some virtual gift certificates he could give to clients who might benefit from my kind of help. He could give them a session with me and there would be no strings attached. I would not attempt to sell them further coaching, or anything else. If they wanted to ask about that it would have to be their idea. Otherwise it would be a pure gift from their accountant.

I knew he knew people who could use some help in the arena of success because he did their books.

He was happy to be able to do this, and as I was leaving the meeting, he asked me a final question:

"Can you help my son? Do the gifted sessions have to be for my business clients?"

Of course I'd talk to his son. He'd just lost a good job and was trying to find a new path in his life.

After a session or two my accountant called to say how much his son loved the experience and that he'd found a new place to work that he really liked. He was sending me two of his clients to have sessions with me.

That's when my own coach's advice hit me: "Talk to who you know. Let them talk to who they know. Let it circle out from there."

I kept doing that. I was finding clients by going through people I already knew. People who already trusted the value of my work.

For example, later on I had an existing client who ran a small internet company, and he was having difficulties with his business partner. We worked on their issues for a few sessions when I asked him, "Do you think it would help if I had a session or two with him?" He said, "Sure, I'm open to anything at this stage. Should I give him two of my sessions?"

I said he didn't have to do that . . . let's just see what I can do.

After the sessions with his partner he saw his attitude start to shift and his communication become more collaborative and less argumentative. The partner really enjoyed the sessions and benefitted from them and asked my client, his boss, if the company would be willing to pay for him to be coached regularly. My client agreed.

Now I had two clients instead of one. I got the second client by going through the first client.

Why had it taken me so long to really see and get that this is a relationship business?

My internal question changed. Whenever I was looking to add another client, I would ask myself, *Who do I know?*

The question I used to be asking myself all day was, *Where are the strangers I'm going to have to bother to see if I can interest them in coaching?*

No wonder I didn't want to do that. No wonder I

procrastinated. No wonder I fell victim to all the marketing approaches being sold to coaches about how they can corral their strangers and turn them into clients by building a funnel of prospects through LinkedIn or other social media, or by learning to podcast, or blog or whatever would get me clients without all those scary conversations and relationships.

Always keep in mind, too, that your own coach can help you. Don't be embarrassed to bring her or him your requests for guidance in choosing who you want to communicate with and how to make the approach in service-oriented ways that don't make you feel pushy or salesy.

I didn't do that at the beginning because I thought my coach would think I lacked courage and initiative. I so admired him that I wanted him to admire me too. That was my ego. Once I switched from seeking his approval to seeking his help, I got all kinds of ideas on how to connect with people in really effective ways based on who I knew and how I could help them.

A key realization here is that people actually enjoy helping other people. They like making a difference. Allow them that enjoyment. And when your ultimate intention is to bring this amazingly life-changing service to the attention of someone who can really use it, it gets easier and easier to drop the adolescent ego game of trying to be liked by everybody. That game and mission, which usually peaks in our high school years, always generates a fear-based life of self-consciousness and personal insecurity—not a great space to come from as a professional coach.

And again, the most effective and helpful way to introduce this "amazingly life-changing service to the attention of someone who can really use it" is through a two-way conversation, not through a one-way impersonal form of self-promotion.

All my failed, one-way promotional activities were done with the idea that of all these people who saw the marketing at least one of them would get the hint and contact me for coaching. But what was being left out of that self-marketing campaign was a way for that one person to know—or to have any idea whatsoever—whether coaching with me would have any value. They may even admire the self-promotion and think, "He's really good at marketing himself and his work!" But, so what? What then?

I had a friend who spent half a year promoting and marketing a book she had written on women and leadership. She spent a lot of time and money on it. She thought it would ultimately get her clients. But when it got her no clients at all, she was discouraged and ready to leave the profession.

The sad thing was that the book was good. She got great reviews and high praise for it. If the leaders who read it had had any clue that she was as good a coach as she was an author, the campaign might have yielded the results she wanted. But how could they have known?

We had a conversation about her discouragement and I asked her, "If the marketing had worked and you were called by a leader asking for coaching, who is someone you'd like that to be?" She named a woman heading up a new company in Austin, Texas, her town.

I said, "Why not take her the book and tell her if she likes it and would like the principles integrated into the company culture she's building, you'll be happy to assist her to do that. You can offer a session or two with her and someone else in her company."

It took her a while and a number of conversations for that leader to experience first-hand that my friend's coaching was even more impactful than the book, which the leader loved, but she ended up with a long-term, well-paid engagement.

You might think I'm describing a technique or specific strategy with that story. But it goes a little deeper than that. The real point is the value of always choosing the direct approach. Living in the now. Connecting with someone today. Not waiting for some long-term, personal branding campaign to eventually get people to take the hint.

The good news here is that anyone can do this. It doesn't require some kind of special personality, or inborn courage, or pre-existing "love of people" for it to work for you and help you get clients.

In the beginning I had more fear of talking to people I didn't know than any coach I've ever met. I had trust issues. I had self-esteem issues. All my activities I was doing to get clients were shot through with anxiety and insecurity.

I felt like any communication I was offering to anyone was me bothering people. It took practice, but the whole nature of my work changed from a day full of trying to get myself to bother people, to seeing who I might be able to help.

Create your own source of built-in happiness. Walk around as a whole, happy person, needing nothing. Then come from this place of wholeness, of self-reliance and independence, and love others. Not because you want them to love you back, not because you want to be needed, but because loving them is an amazing thing to do.

~ Leo Babauta

25.

What if I have no one to talk to?

O ne time very early in my coaching career I went to my coach and said, "I don't have anyone left to talk to to get new clients."

He said "Go print out the last fifty different people who emailed you and print the whole email they sent you. We'll go over them together. It doesn't matter what they emailed you about."

I did just that, and in the next session we looked at the list.

I asked him if we were looking for clients, and he said, "No we're looking for problems or challenges. We're looking for where you can help . . . where you can serve."

His whole life was about service and where he could help. And he never had to look anywhere to get clients.

His practice was always full and his fees were always very high, higher than any coach I knew. And he never had to "look for" clients. People came to him, and after his first few clients he always had a waiting list.

One time he went into his kitchen for lunch and there was a young man in his living room cleaning his carpet. He invited the worker to take a break and sit with him at the kitchen counter. They talked about their jobs, and after my coach talked about his own work as a coach, the carpet cleaner asked what he charged; my coach said, "$150,000 paid up front for a year's work." (He charges more now.)

The carpet cleaner was stunned. A few days later my coach got a call from a dentist in Texas who happened to be the cleaner's brother. He called out of profound curiosity. What kind of "coaching" could possibly merit that kind of fee? My coach told him what happened in the sessions and the kinds of benefits his clients received and the high percentage of his clients who renewed with him year after year.

After a very long conversation about the power of coaching and where the dentist was in his personal and professional life, the dentist asked if he could fly out and get a full experience of that coaching. My coach said yes, and after that two-hour session the wealthy dentist signed up with him for a year.

146 • Steve Chandler

Whenever I told that story to the coaches in our school, some coaches, only half-kidding, said, "So . . . we should all get our carpets cleaned and talk to the cleaner?"

They were looking for a technique. Techniques are one thing (which I covered in the books *The Prosperous Coach*, and *37 Ways to Boost Your Coaching Practice*) but operating principles (which are what this book is attempting to point to) are completely different. Operating principles are even more transformative and effective, because once you have them in a deep way, techniques and strategies come to you all the time. And the beauty of those techniques is that they are the ones that you enjoy and are most likely to get really good at.

Back to my email list.

The first email we looked at was from the owner of the small company who turned my audio recordings into multiple CD copies for me to mail to clients and prospective clients. He was emailing to apologize for not being finished with an overdue job. He said in the email that his business was having some personnel problems and that he was hoping to resolve them soon.

I said, "So we can skip that one."

He said, "Really?"

I said, "I think so . . . What am I missing?

He said, "People who have problems are people you

can help. You have helped people in small businesses, and even written a book about it."

I was slow, but I got it. After the session I called the person and said, "Your company has been a good resource for me for the last couple years, and I'm really grateful for the work you've done for me—always on time. In my work as a coach I help small businesses with problems. If you're open to it, I'll come to your offices and we can brainstorm a bit on your business to see if I can help you with what you're going through."

He said, "I don't know if I can afford you right now, given what we're going through."

I said, "Never mind that for now, let's just see what we can solve."

After a couple hours in their conference room we discovered that their system for recruiting, interviewing and hiring dependable people was no system at all. It was haphazard and half-baked and only used on an emergency basis. It was not in alignment with the owner's desire to create a great little business. We looked at doable ways to strengthen it.

Within weeks they had become a client of mine.

And that was just the first email.

Another email was from a cousin of mine who was regretting that she couldn't come visit as planned, but her husband was having a hard time making his sales goals at his business and the flight was too much money right now.

My coach said, "See anywhere you could help there?"

I offered to help my cousin's husband increase his skills at connecting with potential customers, and although they still couldn't make the trip, after a pro bono month or so his numbers climbed up above his goals and I ended up working with his whole team at my full fee.

Of course not all fifty people led me to clients, but a surprising (to me) number did, and my own operating principle shifted from "looking for clients" over to always looking for where I could help.

If one of my Facebook friends posted about something they were up against or having a problem with, I would private-message them and offer them time to talk about it if they were open to it. Many a private message turned into a long conversation and an eventual request from that person for me to consider taking them on as a client.

If I read in the local paper that a new person had just been appointed to a leadership position, and in the article's interview with them they said what their goal was, or what their intention was—such as, "My intention is to create a culture of trust and high performance and help bring this organization back up to the respect it deserves"—I would communicate with them, tell them I read and admired their interview, and if they were open to it, "I'd be happy to meet and share some ideas that may help you reach those goals."

So it doesn't always have to be a problem I have to find in order to help someone. It can be a goal or any kind of positive challenge. Such as: "I'm trying to be a better father," or "I'm looking to get better at time management." Etc. Etc.

Anywhere I can help.

What we are engaged in creating is the opportunity for people to participate in the transformation of people's lives and of life itself. This context of transformation is a context of freedom and opportunity, of empowerment and human joy, of contribution and of participation.

Participation in this transformation is, for me, the fullest expression of being.

~ **Werner Erhard**

26.

When searching for clients disappears

There are some coaches who have no need whatsoever to read this book.

Why?

They don't need to learn how to get clients.

They already have all the clients they need or want.

And they always will.

And the reason for this is that their practice continuously fills because of two phenomena: renewals and referrals.

In fact, that level of success as a coach is where we are all headed if we stay on the path. Clients who are working with us, a very good percentage of them, will want to keep going, sometimes year after year.

And those clients who are complete with our work and

move on? They leave openings for the clients who are being referred to us to enthusiastically jump into.

Sound too good to be true?

It would have to me in my first years as I was trying to wrangle and wrestle this profession into financial viability and stability.

Today when I am leading a seminar in my school I sometimes tell the coaches that there will come a time, after you've mastered how to get clients, when you won't need that skill anymore. When I say that, I can see the expressions of disbelief on many of their faces.

"How do I speed that process up?" a coach asks, and everyone laughs. As if there couldn't be an easy answer.

But actually there is an answer. Because even though coaching, in most ways, is a profession like no other, in another way, as far as no longer needing to "get clients" is concerned, coaching is a business like any other.

The answer to how a coach keeps a full practice without the constant searching for people is twofold:

1) Referrals

2) Renewals

Notice that neither of these client sources require me to go searching for prospects. Even though we talked about how to ask for help in finding potentials clients (like I did with my accountant), this time we are talking about pure referrals, the ones that come out of the blue with no effort on our part.

Someone emails or messages or says to me, "I have someone who could really use your coaching. Should I have her contact you?"

In my early months of coaching I would say, "Sure, maybe give us an email introduction. I'll take it from there. I'll give her a session or two at no charge to let her get the experience." And then, early me would celebrate the fact that a good prospect was now coming my way. Yay! Right?

Wrong.

Why wrong? Because early me had not yet learned that this is a relationship business . . . not a sales and marketing business.

So I'd wait and wait and nothing would happen.

I'd wonder why this thing called coaching has to be so hard. No wonder my mood is always crashing. Even when I think I've got a good prospect to talk to, someone "who could really use" my coaching, I end up with nothing. This thing called getting clients is like trying to catch fish with my bare hands in a roaring, muddy river!

Over and over, that would happen. I'd complain to my coach about all the so-called referrals that never came through. They didn't even want to take advantage of a free

154 • Steve Chandler

session!

I would say, "It's hard to make a living in a world where people are no damn good."

He would then point out to me (because he was my coach and I always wanted truthful and direct coaching) that in this situation it was I who was no damn good.

"Me?"

"Yes, you. You're still focused on getting instead of giving. You're still focused on reacting instead of creating."

I said, "What am I not creating? I offered time to talk."

"The relationship."

"How can I create a relationship with someone who refuses to talk to me?"

He said that wasn't the person he was talking about.

He was talking about the person doing the referring, the one I'll call the referring party.

And that session was where the "referral triangle" was born. He didn't call it that, but that's what I have called it in all my work with coaches. For years it has helped coaches convert referrals into clients, and at a very high rate of success.

Here's how it works. The moment someone tells me they have someone they'd like to refer to me for possible coaching, I picture a triangle. The three corners of the triangle are the referring party, the prospective client, and me. No one in this triangle is less important than any other.

Why was this a breakthrough in approach? Because most coaches either diminish or totally ignore the importance of the referring party . . . the one who starts the conversation.

In my early days when someone would refer a possible client and I was in my anxious "getting" mindset, I would dismiss them immediately. Immediately they became dead to me. Okay, bye, thanks, get lost, I can't make any money from you, so no need to talk any further.

But, actually? They were the one person in this triangle I did need to talk to.

I needed to expand my relationship with that person and create a good conversation about the person they were referring to me. I had questions:

How well do you know the person you're referring to me?

What's your history together?

Why do you think coaching would benefit her at this time?

Why do you think she has a challenge in that area?

What's been done so far to help her with that issue?

Have you tried to help her?

You seem to care a lot about her getting help. What do you like about her?

What are her best qualities and skills?

If she solves the issue you told me about, what kind of a difference would it make to her in her life?

What kind of opinion do you think she has of coaching itself, and of being coached?

When you introduce us, do you think she'll jump on the chance to have a coaching session or two, or will she tend to hold back?

If she doesn't connect with me and book time with me, would you like me to let you know?

If you're a coach, you can see what I'm doing here. I am building my relationship with my referring party, who is sitting at the top of the triangle. He and I are now forming a partnership together, with a single mission of getting his friend or co-worker some help.

The more he is allowed to talk about how and why he wants her to get help, the more invested he is in actually having that happen. So when he talks to her about the email introduction he is more likely to stress to her that this is a big moment, with the potential to be life-changing.

And now that the two of us have talked for a long time about coaching, but really more about possibility, when I call him to say she has not communicated with me yet, he's most likely going to say, "What? Let me handle this. I'm going to have a real talk with her, and believe me, she will connect with you."

I've had many of those conversations. For someone who's never been coached, or someone whose experience with a coach has been less than relationship-oriented, it can be hard to initiate a call or even agree to an email invite into a session. They are afraid they'll be judged or sold something or both.

There's even a reluctance factor about the offer of a free exploratory session. They often tell me later, "I was almost certain I wouldn't be buying a coaching program, and because of that, I didn't want to have a talk or two with you if I knew it was going to be a waste of time for you."

But in the referral triangle process we address that challenge by helping our referring party understand how we work. We don't see a trial session as a failed sales call. We see it as creating a relationship based on service and creativity. We enjoy the people we talk to who don't hire us as much as the people who do hire us. And many times the people who don't hire us come back later to work with us, or refer someone else to us based on how good the trial sessions were.

So it's never a waste of time. And when the referring party sees this it's easier for him to take that pressure off his friend or co-worker when he's talking to her about the benefits of making this introductory session happen.

A final benefit of focusing on the person doing the referring and creating a good relationship with him is that he'll be likely to refer more people in the future. He will have been more involved in getting his first referral the help she wanted. He will have been an active participant in the triangle.

When you practice this triangle approach you'll be surprised at how easy it is to do. You're not trying to persuade anyone of anything. Your most important conversation is with someone not only happy to talk to you, but also really appreciative of how all of it is based on service. People really want to be a key part of getting someone the help they need.

You don't have to go looking for love when it's where you come from.

~ **Werner Erhard**

27.

From referrals to renewals to prosperity

The better we get as coaches, the more the number of referrals increases. Which is why I always immediately recommend Cal Newport's amazingly wonderful (and useful!) book *So Good They Can't Ignore You* to the coaches I'm working with.

And the more our coaching skills expand and improve, the more our current clients want to renew after our program comes to an end. They just know, based on our experience together so far, that our next round of coaching together will take them to another level.

This is what I was referring to earlier when I said coaching was a business like any other. If you are an attorney whose skills get better and better at winning cases, you'll no longer have to be finding clients. They will be lined up, and your only "problem" will be deciding which cases you *want to* take on.

The same applies to a chef, or a surgeon, or a dentist, or a website designer or an interior decorator (and I could go on ad infinitum).

This might seem obvious when you think about it. But early coaches, including me, get schooled and certified in coaching a certain way; they then consider that part of the profession to be done with and spend all their days looking for clients.

The coaches I know whose whole practices are easily and effortlessly filled with renewals and referrals are always devoting time to learning new and better ways to make a bigger impact in a coaching session. They seek out books, seminars, online programs, retreats given by coaches, and psychologists and spiritual teachers who are at far higher levels than they are—so they can keep learning and growing.

Carol Dweck's brilliant book *Mindset* is based on her exhaustive research that reveals, "People with a fixed mindset—those who believe that abilities are fixed—are less likely to flourish than those with a growth mindset— those who believe that abilities can be developed."

Many coaches have a fixed mindset, especially about their coaching skills. They know how to coach; that's not the problem! They were trained in it at a certification school. Right now, money is the problem.

If you ask them how many of their current clients they think will renew with them, they say, "Renew? What do you mean by that?"

"Continue working with you. Pay their fee for another round."

"Why would they renew? They got what they came for. That's what they tell me."

"Wow, you must be really good."

Well, just kidding. The real reason they didn't renew was that although you made a difference with them, it wasn't a big enough difference to have them want to keep it going.

Your coaching skills will improve in the following ways. These are the best ways I know of. They come from my own experience, and the experience of the many coaches I've known and coached.

1. Being coached

Steve Hardison was my coach long before I had any success at all at coaching. He coached me primarily at the level of being. It wasn't at the level of doing, it was at the level of being. From the beginning it was never really *what are you doing?* The coach was about *who are you being* that is having the *doing* in your life be so ineffective?

When we shifted to who I was being, the right doing would flow from that.

Even when we worked on the doing line, like when he asked me to bring in my emails to find potential clients, that wasn't just a neat trick or technique. He grounded it in being.

Who I was being was a closed-minded pessimist who said, "I don't have anyone to talk to." Once that belief was cleared from me, internally, the external activities I could do opened up.

All the years I've coached with him he has held true to what he first told me, "I coach the person, not the outer world outcome." When people come to him because they want a business or financial outcome, he will acknowledge the doability of that outcome, but then say "I'll be coaching *you*."

And one of his favorite questions he'd ask whenever I brought in a new goal or dream was, "Who would you need to be?" to have that outcome occur.

Being coached so powerfully and impactfully at that depth over the years (as I kept **renewing**) gave me an ongoing "school of one" on how to continuously improve my own skills as a coach.

It was more than obvious to me that **being coached** by

a great coach built my own skills faster than any other thing I did.

2. Coaching others

Every time you coach someone else, you improve as a coach. When you emerge from a coaching session, especially a challenging one, you emerge as a better coach than you were before the session.

That's why newer coaches with easily affordable fees usually become prosperous coaches faster than new coaches who hold out for higher fees.

But how could that make sense? You'd think coaches with higher fees would make more money.

The reason is because the low-fee coach is doing more coaching. They are getting better and better as they go, while the new coach holding out for high fees is giving their full time and anxiety to trying to find the next high fee client.

Many coaches who go to a coaching school look around and hear other coaches talk about how they just got a $50,000 client. They begin to think, "That must be the industry standard!" So they start making bad decisions about what to charge clients.

But one of the many beautiful aspects of this coaching profession is that there are no "industry standards." It's whatever works for you and your clients.

So make sure you are doing a lot of coaching. Especially at the beginning.

Like the leader of the excellent Supercoach Academy, Michael Neill, says, at the beginning of your coaching career "the most important thing is for you to be always coaching. So just coach: coachity, coachity, coach!"

3. Health of the healer

Coaching is the only profession I know of where your own ongoing personal growth and expansion of happiness is a requirement (for optimal success).

Unlike other professions.

A great trial lawyer can have a miserable family life, with ongoing divorces, a secret life of alcoholism, poor health habits and still be a great lawyer that you would hire in a heartbeat to keep you out of prison.

A successful brain surgeon can make millions and be celebrated throughout the medical world and be mean and cruel and miserable in his personal life. (He knows the brain but not the mind or heart.)

A good accountant, a good biologist, a good auto mechanic, a famous actor, a fabulous comedian (like Robin Williams), a great musician (like Elvis . . . like Prince), can all rise to the top of their profession without any attention paid to the wholeness of life.

That won't work for coaches.

Over the past few years I've facilitated a small group of high-fee, successful coaches. We'd meet in person, the five of us, a few weekends a year to sit around a table and coach and mentor each other. The first day was always "Business Day," where we focused on improving our coaching practices and raising our income.

The second day was all about the health of the healer. Mind, body and spirit. Personal relationship challenges. Who we were BEING in the world when we weren't coaching.

It was a little daring for me to ask them to devote a full day to that. Most coaches only want to pay a strong fee for a group like that if it will improve their practice and their income.

But after a week or two, we all were surprised that "Day Two, Spiritual Day" was the most impactful . . . to their coaching success.

If a client brings me problems that I see are being caused by their habitually pessimistic thought pattern (their internal being), it's going to be hard to make a difference with them if I, too, am a pessimist. I could give them *Learned Optimism* by Dr. Martin Seligman or *Positivity* by Dr. Barbara Fredrickson, both excellent books on the subject, but if I myself remain a pessimist, my ability to coach well is almost zero.

So if you want to be "so good they can't ignore you" as a coach, please take care of yourself. Please find ways to keep growing and waking up spiritually (whatever that means to you; do it your way). And in the back of this book I'll provide a list of recommended reading, viewing and listening materials that have helped me on this path. It might not seem, at the logical, intellectual level that it will relate to learning "how to get clients," but I think you'll be pleasantly surprised at how much it ultimately does.

Over the years one of the words I've heard most often when people tell me why they hired their coach is "presence." The coach's presence was something they could immediately feel. In the world of coaching conversations, presence is everything. It's your openness, your focus on the client or prospect, your curiosity, your compassionate listening. It's your *understanding* of the other person. It gives a whole new meaning to the phrase, "how to *get* clients."

Peace is happiness at rest,
and happiness is peace in motion.

~ Wolter Keers

Recommended Resources for Coaches

READING

Loving What Is by Byron Katie

Supercoach by Michael Neill

The Inside-Out Revolution by Michael Neill

Living Service by Melissa Ford

Prison Break by Jason Goldberg

Sweet Sharing by Ankush Jain

Invisible Things by Tina Quinn

Being Human by Amy Johnson

The Little Book of Big Change by Amy Johnson

How to Get the Most out of Coaching by Karen Davis and
    Alex Mill

Fatherhood Is Leadership by Devon Bandison

Wealth Transformation Journal by Kamin Samuel

Accidental Genius by Mark Levy

Untethered Aging by William Keiper

WATCHING (videos online)

Brian Johnson

Byron Katie

George Pransky

Eckhart Tolle

Tom Chi

Dicken Bettinger

Ankush Jain

Jason Goldberg

ONLINE COURSES

The Little School of Big Change (Dr. Amy Johnson)

ACS: The Coaching Prosperity School (Steve Chandler)

Falling in Love with Writing (Michael Neill and Steve Chandler)

Financial Freedom from the Inside-Out (Michael Neill and Steve Chandler)

Bonus Chapters from

Steve Chandler

Introduction: Something better than heaven?

And a hero comes along

Real art comes from the ultimate, from a vision; from the spirit, as Beethoven would say; from God, as Bach would say.

~ Francis Lucille

> Bonus Chapters from
>
> *CREATOR*
>
> by Steve Chandler

INTRODUCTION

Something better than heaven?

There is something better than heaven. It is the eternal, meaningless, infinitely creative mind. It can't stop for time or space or even joy. It is so brilliant that it will shake what's left of you to the depths of all-consuming wonder.

~ Byron Katie

You read that quote and wonder. What is she saying? Does she mean *my* mind? Or does she mean some kind of universal mind? The bottomless well of creativity that Napoleon Hill called "infinite intelligence"? Or is it all the same?

Wouldn't that be exciting, though, to discover something better than heaven and to have that discovery shake me to the depths?

So I wondered how she could say that with such

relaxed certainty. Would she be trying to sell us some new-age product or course? That would be a cynic's view, which is to say it would be *my* view when first I encountered this claim of hers that there was something better than heaven.

A cynic will hear something like this and start to get excited, but then will stop himself. His conditioning has kicked in. What about these bills and these kids to care for? What about all the books and essays I have read by the highly intelligent philosophers of existential despair? Didn't they convince me that the "human condition" was essentially negative?

Yes they did, and it matched up nicely with how I perceived my own condition.

But then things changed, and I began to see that my "condition" was actually only my conditioning.

But what's the difference? Seems like there's no difference.

Here it is: When people like me talk about their "conditioning" they speak of it as if it stopped somewhere. Usually in childhood. That's where conditioning solidifies into the human condition. Or so we're told.

There was conditioning that was caused by what I was taught and how I was raised, and then the conditioning came to completion. After that, for the rest of my life I would be stuck with how I was conditioned. I would refer to it as "my conditioning." It would never change. How could it? It was over and complete.

Inside that story, I had been conditioned just as a piece of meat gets marinated. I'd be sitting in a Polynesian restaurant eating marinated chunks of steak telling you about my childhood and my conditioning as if they were one and the same.

What could be wrong with that story? What is it I didn't know, that if I knew it, might change the game of life forever?

This is what it was:

Conditioning never stops.

Conditioning is ongoing. I'm not marinated meat. I am literally always like a culinary work in progress. Each day is full of possibility. The menu is always new.

Conditioning is continuous. What I did and saw and learned this morning is as vital a part of my ongoing conditioning as the conditioning that occurred in childhood. In fact, today's conditioning is even more vital than my childhood conditioning, especially if it takes me in new directions. Especially when it counters and replaces earlier conditioning.

When I looked back on my life there was more than enough evidence of this. I had been conditioned to believe that drinking alcohol made life better. Then I was conditioned to believe, after I descended into alcoholism, that the only way I could get relief from the pain of living was through drinking and drugs.

But then I joined a program and got a sponsor and created the mental space and spiritual openness for an entirely new conditioning to drop in. This resulted in a total transformation of my relationship to life and people.

And this wasn't childhood. This was my access to ongoing conditioning. Something I didn't know I had. I didn't realize that when it came to conditioning I was now able to assume my rightful role as *creator*. I was now in charge of it. And that wasn't the case in childhood.

So this morning I read the words of Byron Katie and reflect on them. I relax enough to see the truth in them. And I think of my first response to her teaching years ago and understand why it was so pessimistic and dismissive.

People don't change was my core belief. I was stuck with my weaknesses and faults. My job was to try to hide them if I was to have a life. I had to hide—or distract you from—my traits and characteristics. My identity worked against me. And because this was true for me, my first response to Katie was that her words were unreal. (It was a conditioned response.)

But then through a spiritual program of recovery I saw

that I could respond differently. I decided to explore. Byron Katie had devised a little meditative system for the deletion of negative conditioning. She explains it in her first book, *Loving What Is*. She called her system "The Work."

Before I bought her book, I noticed on the cover that Eckhart Tolle had said, "Byron Katie's Work acts like a razor-sharp sword that cuts through . . . illusion and enables you to know for yourself the timeless essence of your being. Joy, peace, and love emanate from it as your natural state. In *Loving What Is*, you have the key. Now use it."

That quote hit me hard because I'd already become a fan of Tolle's book *The Power of Now*. Why would he make that kind of statement? It seemed to go beyond praise for a book. It was as if he was describing a magical garden tool. He wasn't saying how much he enjoyed the book. He was telling me to *use it*.

What would I be digging up?

Well, it turned out to be just about everything. All my old conditioning. All the defeated and pessimistic neural pathways. All the old thoughts mistakenly assumed to be the truth about life.

And why did it work for me? Because I did it. I followed the simple directions. The Work worked just the same way it worked for Katie, as she writes and talks about. She was just sharing what worked for her. She was not putting out some new thing to try to believe in. It will work for you too. And it's not the only path.

Byron Katie had a flash of revelation one morning and saw what so many "enlightened" people have seen (all the great religious figures in the past, on up to Ramana Maharshi, Sydney Banks, Douglas Harding, Werner Erhard, Mooji, Eckhart Tolle, Rupert Spira, Francis Lucille and on and on). She saw life as pure love and light.

But then her thoughts started coming back in. All the old conditioning. So she *created* her system she called The Work. It worked for her. It revealed thought to be what it was, and so thought was no longer the great truth about life. And she promised everyone she worked with and taught her system to that if they were courageous enough to stay with it to the very end, they too would see clearly that "There is something better than heaven. It is the eternal, meaningless, infinitely creative mind."

Hers is but one path back to the realization and occupation of the infinitely creative mind. There are many others, both spiritual and psychological. I'll put some of the most effective books and teachers in the *Recommended Reading* section at the end. These are based on my own experience and the experience of people I work with.

My clients want to believe in what Katie sees and what Syd Banks and Ramana Maharshi and other spiritual philosophers saw. But their conditioning keeps chattering the old pessimistic mantras. And I can relate to them completely. I wanted to believe, too. I would listen to Alan Watts say, "No valid plans for the *future* can be made by those who have no *capacity* for living now," and I would think, "Okay there go my plans for the future. And I thought the future was going to save me."

I was wanting to believe I could experience joy and creativity in living now, but I wasn't seeing that it was not a matter of belief. It was a matter of experience.

When I was a little boy I wanted to believe the deep end of the pool water would hold me up, but my conditioned thought chatter said, "Don't go there, you're heavier than water."

My mistake was staying stuck inside wanting to believe deep water would hold me up. I didn't realize that belief had nothing to do with it. In fact, belief and disbelief were the things that were holding me back. Stalling things out. Familiarity with the water was all I needed in order to reveal the truth of it.

Both believers and non-believers (in my head) can step aside as I jump in. They are only in the way.

To live in the world of creation—to get into it and stay in it—to frequent it and haunt it—to think intently and fruitfully—to woo combinations and inspirations into being by a depth and continuity of attention and meditation—this is the only thing.

~ Henry James

And a hero comes along

Throughout my boyhood I loved comic book superheroes, as so many children do. Mighty Mouse, Superman, and Captain Marvel filled my dreams. I had the comic books and watched the TV episodes and always felt a surge of excitement picturing myself with their powers.

When I began growing into adulthood the superheroes lost their pull. Adulthood was getting harder and harder for me to navigate, and those old heroes were just fantasies, right? I needed to get into reality. (One thesaurus I looked at recently had a lot of synonyms for the word *creativity* but only one antonym. The antonym they listed was "*reality.*")

I needed to deal with my lack of power that seemed to accompany growing up.

That was the thinking that was circulating inside me back then. And when my not-so-super life of bad choices got too heavy to hold up, I finally hit bottom. I found myself in recovery meetings for alcoholics where we admitted we were powerless over alcohol and that our lives had become unmanageable. I had become Powerless Man. A long way from Superman.

Or so I thought at the time.

But then, little by little, with recovery adding more light each day, I began to wake up. I was free of addiction for the first time and the world began to open up in front of me. More and more often I found myself in good spirits. I was attending meetings about spiritual recovery in which we explored and practiced "conscious contact with a higher power." It was all new to me. But it was real, practical experience. Not just something one hopes for.

It was truly recovery . . . not just from alcohol but from what my meetings called "self-will run riot." It felt like the ego was fading out while the light of recovery unfolded like a blanket of stars.

It wasn't until much later that I saw that my (and our) higher power (the God of our understanding) was creativity itself.

Before it made its real appearance, I had always liked the *word* "creativity," and I had bought into the prevailing belief that it was a rare and precious thing. I also noticed that my ego really liked it when people said I, as an individual personality, was creative. Really? You mean that? I took it very personally. I remember being extremely proud of myself when I was named "Creative Director" of an advertising agency. How special it felt to be seen as creative! And not just creative, but so creative that they want you to be the *Director* of creativity! I was captivated by how *unique* I was becoming and—really—how exceptional I must be! I guess I'll just have to learn to accept that I'm *one of the rare few* who have access to this form of magic we all call creativity!

But my thoughts weren't really matching up with reality. Deep down I knew it. My belief (and the belief of those around me) that creativity was an uncommon personal gift began to lose its credibility. I could soon see that it was a story, like so many of my other stories, designed to keep the ego feeling unique. But it had nothing to do with real creativity. Or real and true reality—no matter what my thesaurus and my culture said.

The more spiritual work and study I did the more I saw that creativity and the life force were one and the same. And it was a force running through everybody, not just the chosen creative few. In our recovery meetings we all had a higher power, higher than the ego, and higher than human thought.

Here we were, a group of alcoholics and drug addicts sitting together trying to learn to live a normal, clean and sober life . . . and one sign on the meeting hall wall said, "Your best thinking got you here."

We weren't sages; we were drunks. But we were experiencing the same kind of higher power that the sages wrote about. A power without upper limits. You could call it a superpower—just what I longed for as a kid. Maybe my yearning and longing and reaching out for Superman as a boy was not a total delusion.

If I wrote an adventure comic book today I would see if I could introduce a new superhero—which would be no small thing given how many superheroes there already are: Wonder Woman, Iron Man, Supergirl, Daredevil, Batman, and you know we could go on.

My comic book's superhero would be you.

I know that's not a really exciting or marketable name for a superhero. "You!"

No, so let's call you something else. How about this. Do you know how movies always acknowledge the "creator" of various superhero characters? For example, Wonder Woman's creator was William Marston. Imagine how powerful he must have been. It's one thing to be Wonder Woman, but it's quite another to be able to *create* Wonder Woman.

If these characters like Wonder Woman and Superman and Mighty Mouse are so powerful, just imagine how much more powerful their creators must be. That's the ultimate superpower right there: the ability to create.

I'd call that hero "Creator."

And the adventures I'd present would show you that it's all based on a true story: the story of you.

About the author

Steve Chandler is the author and co-author of over thirty books published in dozens of languages around the world.

He is the founder of the Coaching Prosperity School (the ACS), which has taught hundreds of coaches from around the world for a decade and a half the principles and systems behind creating a prosperous practice. His newest book, *How to Get Clients*, describes the inner ways of being that will lead a coach to financial success based on the work done in the Coaching Prosperity School.

Chandler has been a corporate leadership and sales trainer for over 50 Fortune 500 companies, and his books *The Joy of Selling*, *100 Ways to Motivate Others*, and *The Hands-Off Manager* reflect the content of his work in that arena.

He currently lives in Birmingham, Michigan with his wife, Kathy, and two hellhounds: Jimmy and Hastings.

Books by Steve Chandler

How to Get Clients: New Pathways to Coaching Prosperity
CREATOR
RIGHT NOW
Death Wish
Crazy Good
37 Ways to BOOST Your Coaching Practice
Wealth Warrior
Time Warrior
Fearless
Shift Your Mind Shift the World (revised edition)
50 Ways to Create Great Relationships
The Prosperous Coach (with Rich Litvin)

Audio by Steve Chandler

9 Lies That Are Holding Your Business Back
10 Habits of Successful Salespeople
17 Sales Lies
37 Ways to BOOST Your Coaching Practice (audiobook)
Are You A Doer Or A Feeler?
Challenges
Choosing
Crazy Good (audiobook)
CREATOR (audiobook)
Creating Clients
Creative Relationships
Death Wish (audiobook)
Expectation vs. Agreement
Fearless (audiobook)
Financially Fearless
How To Double Your Income As A Coach
How to Get Clients (revised edition) (audiobook)
How To Help A Pessimist
How To Solve Problems
Information vs. Transformation
Is It A Dream Or A Project?
Making A Difference
MindShift: The Steve Chandler Success Course
Ownership And Leadership
People People
Personality Reinvented
Purpose vs. Personality
Reflections on RelationShift: Major-Gift Fundraising

RIGHT NOW (audiobook)
Serving vs. Pleasing People
Shift Your Mind Shift the World (revised edition) (audiobook)
Testing vs. Trusting
The Creating Wealth audio series
The Fearless Mindset
The Focused Leader
The Function Of Optimism
The Joy Of Succeeding
The Most Powerful Client Attractor
The Owner / Victim Choice
The Prosperous Coach (audiobook)
The Ultimate Time Management System
Time Warrior (audiobook)
Wealth Warrior (audiobook)
Welcoming Every Circumstance
Who You Know vs. What You Do
Why Should I Reinvent Myself?
You'll Get What You Want By Asking For It

Steve Chandler Coaching Prosperity School

Steve's world-acclaimed ACS (Advanced Client Systems) is now available as an online masterclass at a tenth of the cost of the original program.

Check out all the features and content of the *Steve Chandler Coaching Prosperity School* on Steve's website, www.stevechandler.com

- Learn to convert your coaching skills into prosperity.
- Hear our powerful guest teachers share their insights and secrets to getting clients and creating a financially thriving practice.
- You'll learn from Steve Chandler and great coaches like Rich Litvin, Carolyn Freyer-Jones, Michael Neill, Karen Davis, Ron Wilder and many more . . . all graduates of the Coaching Prosperity School.

- Over 30 full video lessons and more than 50 short video tips, plus bonus audio programs to build your coaching practice.

"This man has changed—and continues to change—my life! One of the reasons that I am the coach I am today is because of his wisdom and leadership.

"Seeing him model masterful coaching and transformational living and practice building through the Coaching Prosperity School program was one of the most insightful and empowering experiences of my life.

"If you are a coach who is committed to greatness in building your practice without internet marketing tactics or having to have a huge mailing list or Twitter followers, AND get the results from yourself that are required to truly be prosperous, being a part of Steve Chandler's new program may be the greatest investment you ever make in yourself."

~ **Jason Goldberg,** master coach and author of *Prison Break*

GO HERE to learn more:

www.stevechandler.com

MAURICE BASSETT

Publisher's Catalogue

The Mahatma Gandhi Library

#1 Towards Non-Violent Politics

* * *

The Prosperous Series

#1 The Prosperous Coach: Increase Income and Impact for You and Your Clients (Steve Chandler and Rich Litvin)

#2 The Prosperous Hip Hop Producer: My Beat-Making Journey from My Grandma's Patio to a Six-Figure Business (Curtiss King)

#3 The Prosperous Hotelier (David Lund)

* * *

Devon Bandison

Fatherhood Is Leadership: Your Playbook for Success, Self-Leadership, and a Richer Life

Roy G. Biv

1921: A Celebration of Toned 1921 Peace Dollars as Numismatic Art

Dancing on Antique Toning: A Further Celebration of Numismatic Art

Dancing on Rainbows: A Celebration of Numismatic Art
Early Jackie: The "Lost" Photos of Jackie Bouvier

Sir Fairfax L. Cartwright

The Mystic Rose from the Garden of the King

Steve Chandler

37 Ways to BOOST Your Coaching Practice: PLUS: the 17 Lies That

Hold Coaches Back and the Truth That Sets Them Free

50 Ways to Create Great Relationships

Business Coaching (Steve Chandler and Sam Beckford)

Crazy Good: A Book of CHOICES

CREATOR

Death Wish: The Path through Addiction to a Glorious Life

Fearless: Creating the Courage to Change the Things You Can

How to Get Clients: New Pathways to Coaching Prosperity

The Prosperous Coach: Increase Income and Impact for You and Your
    Clients (The Prosperous Series #1) (Steve Chandler and Rich Litvin)

RIGHT NOW: Mastering the Beauty of the Present Moment

Shift Your Mind Shift The World (Revised Edition)

Time Warrior: How to defeat procrastination, people-pleasing, self-
    doubt, over-commitment, broken promises and chaos

Wealth Warrior: The Personal Prosperity Revolution

Kazimierz Dąbrowski

Positive Disintegration

Charles Dickens

A Christmas Carol: A Special Full-Color, Fully-Illustrated Edition

Melissa Ford

Living Service: The Journey of a Prosperous Coach

M. K. Gandhi

Towards Non-Violent Politics (The Mahatma Gandhi Library #1)

James F. Gesualdi

Excellence Beyond Compliance: Enhancing Animal Welfare Through the
    Constructive Use of the Animal Welfare Act

Janice Goldman

Let's Talk About Money: The Girlfriends' Guide to Protecting Her ASSets

Sylvia Hall

This Is Real Life: Love Notes to Wake You Up

Christy Harden

Guided by Your Own Stars: Connect with the Inner Voice and Discover Your Dreams

I ♥ Raw: A How-To Guide for Reconnecting to Yourself and the Earth through Plant-Based Living

Curtiss King

The Prosperous Hip Hop Producer: My Beat-Making Journey from My Grandma's Patio to a Six-Figure Business (The Prosperous Series #2)

David Lindsay

A Blade for Sale: The Adventures of Monsieur de Mailly

Rich Litvin

The Prosperous Coach: Increase Income and Impact for You and Your Clients (The Prosperous Series #1) (Steve Chandler and Rich Litvin)

David Lund

The Prosperous Hotelier (The Prosperous Series #3)

John G. W. Mahanna

The Human Touch

Abraham H. Maslow

The Aims of Education (audio)

The B-language Workshop (audio)

Being Abraham Maslow (DVD)

The Eupsychian Ethic (audio)

The Farther Reaches of Human Nature (audio)

Maslow and Self-Actualization (DVD)

Maslow on Management (audiobook)

Personality and Growth: A Humanistic Psychologist in the Classroom

Psychology and Religious Awareness (audio)

The Psychology of Science: A Reconnaissance

Self-Actualization (audio)

Weekend with Maslow (audio)

Harold E. Robles

Albert Schweitzer: An Adventurer for Humanity

Albert Schweitzer

Reverence for Life: The Words of Albert Schweitzer

Patrick O. Smith

ACDF: The Informed Patient: My journey undergoing neck fusion surgery

William Tillier

Personality Development through Positive Disintegration: The Work of Kazimierz Dąbrowski

Margery Williams

The Velveteen Rabbit: or How Toys Become Real

Made in the USA
Las Vegas, NV
22 April 2021